What Makes Things Happen

What Makes Things Happen

Luck, Chance, Fate—or Freedom?

KIM TREIGER-BAR-AM

RESOURCE *Publications* · Eugene, Oregon

Resource Publications
An Imprint of Wipf and Stock Publishers
199 W. 8th Ave., Suite 3
Eugene, OR 97401

www.wipfandstock.com

PAPERBACK ISBN: 979-8-3852-5175-9
HARDCOVER ISBN: 979-8-3852-5176-6
EBOOK ISBN: 979-8-3852-5177-3

VERSION NUMBER 06/09/25

I dedicate this book to my parents

Contents

Introduction

DO WE HAVE CONTROL over the events in our lives? Are the paths we follow determined by an external force on high, such as God, fate, or the stars? Is every effect preceded by a cause, or do events occur by the whims of chance? These questions have been debated for centuries, both in Jewish tradition and across various cultures. Greek mythology, for example, which is widely infused in the West, depicts goddesses known as the Fates spinning fabric on a wheel, setting the texture of our lives.

For many, luck, chance, and fate are forces that shape our lives. But there's another view: that we fashion our own lives. We make our own luck. We take the chances open to us, and realize opportunities that come our way. We decide our own fate. This belief is part of Jewish tradition, and resonates deeply in the modern world as well.

Most of us live with a feeling that there are forces outside of our control and also the freedom to make choices that affect our lives. It's as if we're caught between being controlled by something greater than ourselves and the power to make decisions and operate.

The central question here is: what really determines our path in life? Is it luck, chance, or fate? In this book, I argue that it's our freedom that truly guides our way. We are free agents, able to shape our own future. The question isn't why things happen—which we'll never really know—but what makes the paths in our life go on their way.

External influences in our lives such as family, friends, community, societal norms, and ideologies certainly affect us. Some of us also believe that they have a *telos,* a purpose, perhaps a Divine mission sent from on high or from tradition. But even these attachments and beliefs are choices we make. Ultimately, it is we who decide, and we who act. Every one of us has freedom, and the power of human agency.

The key takeaway is this: use your freedom affirmatively and responsibly. At the same time, be aware of the forces that shape you, and give thanks for them. We are not alone.

The book highlights three areas where action is needed: climate change, the proposed judicial overhaul in Israel, and the current war.

The planet is facing the devastating effects of climate change. Whether we think of it as a natural cycle or a man-made disaster, it's affecting us all. We must make efforts now to prevent further environmental damage.

Israel's governing coalition proposed an overhaul of the judicial system, which sparked raging protests in recent years. The protests were largely successful; they managed to thwart many of the coalition's efforts. However, the governing coalition continues to push for the regime overhaul. This must be stopped. Democratic checks and balances must be preserved.

Israelis have been thrust into an incredibly difficult situation, with the launching of the current war. But the response has been nothing short of extraordinary. The resilience and "get-up-and-go" of the people have been inspiring. They've shown the strength of human agency in the face of adversity.

In some of these situations, an attitude of passivity has been suggested. Climate change is simply nature's course, it has been said; the fall of democracy is what the people want; and anti-Semitism is inevitable. Yet with the strength that freedom affords us, with a commitment to responsible action, we can defy these passive views. *We can make things happen.*

A key lesson is the power of hope. This is the theme of Israel's national anthem, *Hatikvah* (התקווה): "The Hope." Hope is a force for change.

So, *act*. We can make things happen.

CHAPTER SUMMARIES

Chapter one talks about luck. "*Mazel*" is the Yiddish term used in many countries around the world to refer to luck. The Hebrew term "*mazal*," carrying the same meaning, is used here. We'll look to how luck is understood in Jewish tradition and other cultures around the world, including Asian practices. It is seen that there is even a notion of making your own luck, and creating your own *mazal*.

What about chance? Chapter two explores how we think of chance in both scientific and everyday terms. It turns out that many of the so-called random events we experience are actually shaped by our choices and actions. What happens to us isn't wholly about statistics; it's influenced by the way we behave.

Discussion in the third chapter focuses on *goral*, the Hebrew word for fate. In Israel, especially with the ongoing war, *goral* is a compelling concept. While some see fate as beyond their control, like it is in the classic Greek sense and often in modern times, in Jewish tradition, *goral* is open to one's own making. Zionism, for example, embodies the idea of taking control of your fate through collective effort.

Finally, we'll explore the concept of freedom. In view are two of my previous books: *Positive Freedom and the Law*, and *Freedom and Respect in Jewish Ethics*. Drawing on Western philosophy and Jewish tradition, we'll look at how freedom allows us to make things happen. We can make our own luck, take chances, and craft our fate. Freedom gives us the power to shape of our lives, and fix the world.

1

Luck

LUCK IS SOMETHING WE hear about everywhere. It is in movies, songs and everyday conversations. Frank Sinatra's classic song "Luck Be a Lady Tonight," from a film years ago, still sticks with us, expressing a wish for good fortune. More recent examples of luck showing up in pop culture include the film *Just My Luck* and the music videos "Lucky Girl Syndrome" and "I'm So Lucky." In Jewish culture the song "*Mazel Tov*," meaning "good luck," is repeatedly sung at joyful occasions.

Luck is ordinarily seen as a force that makes things happen. It is said to be the reason something happened, or anyway is used to explain the event's occurrence. We want to think that there is a reason for everything. Something must cause things to happen; that's cause and effect. So we will say it is luck. But we don't really know.

Luck is a way of dealing with uncertainty. When something unexpected happens, we might say: "It was just luck." Time and again people say this with a shrug of the shoulders, and it serves as a quick way of saying, "Who knows?" It is a manner of accepting life's mysteries. We might wonder why something happened, but never know the full answer.

Where does luck come from? Maybe luck is indeed something out there, an invisible force that affects us. Maybe some people are simply born lucky, or luck attaches itself to certain individuals. Superstitions and rituals are thought to bring luck your way.

This chapter explores the different intuitions people have about luck. We'll focus on cultural customs that are thought to bring good fortune. While practices in the Jewish tradition are the focus, we'll also touch on other cultures, including Asian rites. The following section surveys the meanings of the term luck. In the final section of this chapter the sources of luck are reflected upon: is luck a gift from God, or the stars? Or is it something we create ourselves in freedom, through our actions?

CUSTOMS

In delving into the different ways people think about luck, it's important to look at the customs of luck and the beliefs tied to them. These symbols, generally fun and jubilant, are common across many cultures.

Around the world, there are signs and sayings that are thought to bring good fortune. The belief that unseen forces, whether from the heavens or elsewhere, can impact our lives is something people share globally. We'll start by looking at the Jewish heritage and then inquire into other cultures.

Jewish Tradition

Mazal in Jewish culture represents the belief in a hidden force that shapes people's lives. The word *"mazel"* is the Yiddish term used around the world to mean "luck." In Hebrew and in Israel, the common term is *"mazal,"* which is used in discussion here for the focus on the Jewish heritage and Israel.

The conception of *mazal* has been part of Jewish thought for centuries. It suggests that our world is touched by, or perhaps even governed by, a force beyond our comprehension. This belief in *mazal* is deeply ingrained in Jewish communities and is reflected in rituals passed down through generations.

One of the most familiar expressions relating to *mazal* is the saying *"Mazal tov,"* which is translated as "Good luck." This phrase is repeatedly used to express joy and congratulations on the happy occasions of weddings, as well as bar/bat mitzvahs, when a child reaches adulthood. The song *"Simen tov, mazal tov"* is regularly sung at these events. Its first word, *simen,* means "sign," underscoring that *mazal* is a sign or symbol of good fortune.

Jewish practices, both ancient and modern, underscore the strong influence that *mazal* holds in people's lives. One well-known custom is the tying of red strings to the doorposts of homes, or wearing and displaying the *hamsa,* which is a palm-shaped amulet meant to ward off the evil eye. The word *hamsa* refers to the five fingers of the hand, and in Mizrahi (Eastern) traditions the phrase *"hamsa, hamsa, hamsa"* is commonly used to protect against bad luck. In Ashkenazi (Western European) traditions, people say *"poo poo poo"* while waving their hands to ward off the evil eye.

Even prayer shows this. By placating or appeasing the spirits, one is deemed to be able to affect one's life path.

Ultimately, these habits show human agency: by the individual engaging in prayer, the person is deemed to be able to affect occurrences and effect outcomes.

Mazal also extends to symbols like the wheel of fortune. In Hebrew, the term for the Zodiac using the term *mazal* is גלגל המזלות (*galgal ha-mazalot*), which translates to "wheel of the constellations," and is closely associated with *mazal*. This is reflected in ancient Jewish art, for instance in the mosaic tiles in synagogues that depict Zodiac signs.

The circular nature of the wheel of fortune, the Hebrew *galgal hamazalot*, and the Zodiac all reflect how life is thought to move in cycles, where what goes around comes around. Even in popular culture this notion is echoed. Recall the song by Joni Mitchell taken from the Proverbs associated with the ancient King Solomon, regarding seasons going round and round.

These customs reflect a deep-rooted trust in *mazal*, or at the very least an acknowledgement of its influence. The prevalence of these rituals indicates a widespread notion that a person can influence the course of their life. Efforts to either celebrate good *mazal* or avert bad *mazal* suggest the presumption of external forces impacting us, and that we can affect them. Rites can turn bad luck to good.

The Golem Myth

The myth of the Golem shows how we assume there are forces beyond our control affecting what happens to us, and also highlights the role humans play in protecting themselves. It's a story about both external and internal forces. It is not in fact about luck, but is relevant here since it is about forces and how they can be deemed both good and bad, both delightful and threatening.

4

The "Golem" is a mythical figure from Jewish folklore, said to have been created from clay of the earth by Rabbi Loew of Prague (known as the *Maharal*) back in the 16th century. The Golem was created to protect the Jewish people in Prague. According to the legend, the Golem was fashioned by human hands to aid humanity.

The Golem followed all of the commands it was given, and helped a great deal around the town. But one Sabbath it did not have a rest: the Rabbi forgot to remove the note inscribing Holy words from its mouth or forehead, which breathed life into it. As a result, the Golem went wild and caused chaos.

This myth encapsulates the dual aspects of delight and threat, similar to the Jewish concept of *mazal*. The Golem, akin to good and bad *mazal*, is a source of both joy and of danger. Today, the element of delight continues with "Golem cookies" being sold as tourist souvenirs in Prague. And in modern Hebrew, the term "Golem" is used jokingly to describe someone who's a bit clueless or helpless.

In some stories we see a female Golem. In modern times, Cynthia Ozick's *Puttermesser Papers* depicts a Golem in New York City. In that story the Golem is a woman created by a woman, in a novel written by a woman. This taps into feminist theories of creation and domination. Also Greek mythology represents a mix of threat and delight in depictions of the female goddesses known as the Fates spinning the wheel of life.

The danger of the Golem is clear when it becomes destructive. It's similar to the Frankenstein story, about a creature made by humans that turns on its creator. These myths remind us that powerful figures, whether Divine or human, carry the potential both for creation and for destruction.

Today, we see a similar fear in the rise of artificial intelligence, as something humans create that could spiral into chaos. Ultimately, the Golem symbolizes society's fear of creation getting out of hand. But it also reflects the hope that we can fix things before they go too far.

Asian Customs

Luck is also present in Chinese, Korean and other Asian cultures. In Chinese culture, for instance, luck is a pervasive theme, as is illustrated in Amy Tan's *The Joy Luck Club*, where trust in fortune is woven throughout the characters' lives. Some of the Asian rituals regarding luck are similar to those in the West and in Jewish practice.

An element shared between both Asian and Jewish customs is the use in both cultures of hanging red strings to ward off the evil eye, basically bad energy or bad luck. Asian and Jewish traditions view these symbols as safeguards, similar to other practices like kissing a *mezuzah*—parchment inscribed with verses from the Torah and hung on doorposts—for Jews, or kissing a cross for Christians, or even kissing dice before rolling them, or praying. These practices are presumed to be protective, and to call forth higher powers or good spirits.

Related to luck, or perhaps more a matter of fate, is the practice of hoping to affect destined love. The Jewish notion of *Beshert* recalls the determination from forces on high of a match meant to be. Couples who unite sometimes say or it is said about them that their meeting was *Beshert*. That is a Yiddish term based on German, with the meaning that their being a couple was destined. A Talmudic story tells of a heavenly voice proclaiming who someone's future spouse will be 40 days before they're born.

This connects with the Korean concept of *"in-yun,"* which suggests that past-life connections determine future relationships. The 2023 film *Past Lives* brings up this notion, showing how what an individual does in this life can change the course of their love story, even if it alters what seems to have been already decided by fate. The film hints that while *in-yun* may be affected by an external force, perhaps in addition it depends upon occurrences that people initiate.

Also the Buddhist notion of *"karma"* points to one's behavior now (or in past lives) affecting your future. This belief has been adopted across various Asian cultures. *Karma* shows that an external force is at work in how your life turns out, but also that it is caused by what we do in present or past lives. The Buddhist concept of *karma* further blurs the lines between external forces and personal agency.

Jewish thought has something similar with *rahamim*, or compassion. There's a Talmudic story about Rabbi Akiva's daughter being saved from a venomous snake bite on her wedding night after she gave her wedding feast to a poor hungry man (Babylonian Talmud ("BT")-Shabbat 156b). The story shows that our kindness can have a powerful effect on our lives and the future.

Other Traditions

Various cultures incorporate concepts involving external forces beyond our control, akin to luck. The Christian ritual mentioned above of kissing a cross can be seen as both a safety technique and as recognizing a higher force.

Christian views of luck and fate have been prevalent throughout history. These beliefs appear in modern theology and the writings of figures including Calvin and Luther, among many others. While these theories are not expounded upon here, it is important to recognize that the notion of external forces including God or gods is present in numerous heritages. At the same time, it's important to recall that some branches of Christianity honor the idea that humans have the freedom to shape their own life path.

Ancient Greek mythology contains references to external spirits, with gods and goddesses influencing human fortunes. Tyche (or Fortuna in Latin), the Greek goddess of luck, fortune, chance, and fate, is one such figure. She is typically shown blindfolded, symbolizing how unpredictable luck can be; you never know when it's going to favor you. Sometimes Tyche is standing on a ball, which further emphasizes how uncertain fortune can be. Tyche is still present in Italian culture today, reinforcing the belief that luck plays a big role in one's life. She has been compared to the popular Indian goddess Lakshmi (Sri), who is also associated with luck and prosperity.

Women are time and again seen as managing one's life. The view that women influence one's luck or fate is seen in the song "Luck Be a Lady Tonight," in which luck itself is personified as a woman. Women are simultaneously perceived as both a threat and a source of delight, as is luck itself.

Interestingly, the Roman goddess Fortuna is depicted as a woman, and she frequently holds a wheel of fortune. This image brings to mind Vanna White, the female TV personality who spun the *Wheel of Fortune* for years. Also the Greek goddesses known as the Moirai, or Fates, are portrayed as women weaving the story of someone's life and determining their fate.

There's a further human element in these heritages, as well. For instance Virgil writes that fortune favors the bold, which suggests that the brave and daring are more liable to attract good luck. Perhaps this is echoed in *Julius Caesar*, where Shakespeare writes: "There is a tide in the affairs of men . . . which leads on to fortune . . . And we must take the current when it serves, or lose our ventures." How humans act is a key part of how our fortune plays out.

The Jewish view of fate differs from the deterministic and inescapable Greek notion, as discussed in Chapter 3.

Other practices, such as fortune-telling, also try to predict or influence the future. Reading tea leaves, Tarot cards, astrology, and the Zodiac are all ways people try to understand what luck has in store for them. Palmistry, or examining the lines on one's hand, is another example. These methods suggest that external forces are at play in guiding our lives, but there's an interesting twist: in palmistry, it's the palm of *your* own hand that's being read. Astrology looks at the date when *you* were born. It's a reminder that forces affecting your life might be both external and deeply personal.

THE MEANING OF LUCK

Luck, as well as the Hebrew term *mazal*, is seen as a force that shapes events. It makes things happen. *Mazal* is typically associated with good things happening. The force is generally deemed to be external, rather than directly a result of one's conduct. Yet there is also a notion of making your own luck. In popular culture, especially on platforms including TikTok, terms such as *manifestation*, *shifting to an alternate reality*, and *wishfulness* have become trendy, suggesting that individuals can influence their fortunes.

The word *mazal* is sometimes used reflexively in Hebrew, as in *hitmazel mazali*. This term means that good luck or fortune has come through. Yet today, use of this reflexive form seems to reflect the feeling that people take part in making their own luck. At the same time, it's also a way of acknowledging the external force that helps bring that luck to life. The term gives thanks.

Philosopher Ludwig Wittgenstein says that the meaning of a word is shaped by how it is used. Indeed by looking at how people use the words luck and *mazal*, we can gain deeper insight into how people think about and interact with fortune.

What Happens

The word *mazal* points to past, present, and future. *Mazal* describes how things turned out, how they're going now, and how they might unfold down the road. *Mazal* is also a way to indicate why something happens. It signals that we just don't know. The reference to luck or *mazal* leaves room for uncertainty. They are open-ended.

Judaism doesn't shy away from acknowledging uncertainty. The Torah uses two terms for law: *chok* and *mishpat* (חוק, משפט). The first is a law without a stated reason. These laws point to uncertainty. Sages explain that if we sought reasons for these laws, we would not understand them. The second term refers to laws with reasons that we can attempt to understand. Hence only sometimes can we even try to comprehend it (namely when it is a *mishpat* rather than a *chok*). The distinction between these two kinds of laws brings out that some things are simply beyond our understanding.

Judaism acknowledges other forms of uncertainty, and things we cannot grasp. For instance, the patriarch Abraham is said to have faced ten tests, one of which was learning to live with uncertainty. In the Torah narrative of the binding of Isaac, Abraham is called by God to take his son "to a place I will show you." The location of that place was not defined. Abraham had to trust that God would reveal the place when the time came. The Hebrew word used in the Torah for "the place" is *hamakom*, which is also a name for God ("*HaMakom*"). When Abraham awoke the morning after receiving the Divine command, he dressed, saddled his donkey, and embarked on a journey without knowing his destination. By accepting the uncertainty, Abraham met the test

A figure's moving forward without knowing the exact destination also comes up in an earlier story in the Torah, in the chapter *Lech Lecha* (Genesis 12:1). God tells Abraham to leave his home and journey to the land that God will show him. The theme of stepping into the unknown is central in this chapter, where God encourages Abraham to keep going even when he doesn't have all the answers.

Threat or Delight

Luck is something that seems to swing this way and that. It resembles the tick-tock of a clock, as we will see with chance and fate, as well. The image of a spinning wheel will pop up again and again throughout the book. Luck can denote unexpected surprises or events, whether good or bad. But usually when people talk about luck, they are referring to something good. While luck can be both a threat and a delight, it's mostly used to describe something positive. The word "serendipity" is another term used for unexpected good fortune. Interestingly, the German words for luck and happiness are quite similar to each other.

In Jewish culture, the phrase *mazal tov* is used quite often, especially during celebrations. The song "*simen tov, mazal tov*" evokes auspicious signs of good fortune, reinforcing the connection between *mazal* and favorable outcomes. *Mazal* is a way of acknowledging that something good has happened. Saying "*mazal sheh*" is akin to saying "I'm lucky that . . ." or "It's a good thing that . . ." when something fortunate occurs.

As a colloquial expression of something positive, *mazal* can refer to skill. Someone shared with me the observation that when an arrow hits its target, someone might exclaim "*mazal!*" *Mazal* here means that you are lucky that the arrow happened to hit the target, or acknowledges your skill in making the shot. Some would say that skill is itself a matter of luck. Namely, it is the luck of being born with a natural ability that others don't have. In his critique of meritocracy, political philosopher Michael Sandel argues that success recurrently comes down to luck: luck in the abilities you're born with, and luck in the socioeconomic circumstances that enable those abilities to flourish. But skill is also honed through hard work and practice. It's about taking up opportunities (discussed in Chapter 2) and exercising free agency (explored in Chapter 4). Whether it's something you're born with or something you develop, skill is undoubtedly a valuable trait.

People talk about *mazal* in finding the right job or partner, too. It's seen as a sign of good fortune, something that feels destined or meant to be. We'll talk more about destiny in Chapters 3 and 4.

Mazal can also be bad. The Hebrew phrase about the evil of luck (*roah hamazal*) suggests that luck can take a turn for the worse. The expression also regarding bad *mazal* stating "it was bad luck that . . ." (*le-roah hamazal*) reflects the uneasy feeling we get when life feels uncertain or unpredictable. It's about not knowing where life's path is taking us or what forces are out there influencing us, and whether our own behavior might lead to something unfortunate.

There's also a phrase about the evil of a decree *(roah gzar hadin)*, which refers to a harsh judgment or decision that falls on someone. The phrase does not include the word *mazal*, but it also suggests that external forces may shape our fate, negatively. Yet the phrase carries a connotation of personal responsibility as well. Such a decree typically comes because of something we've done, as a law or rule applies to us based on our behavior.

As Wittgenstein suggests, we can look at the use of a word to see its meaning, and by the use of *mazal* we see that it points to the forces shaping our lives as both external and internal. *Mazal* might seem to reflect something out of our control, but it can also reflect the choices we make and things we do. *Mazal* can point to free agency. Even where it is deemed to be bad, the *mazal* that falls upon someone may be a sign of choices they have made and ways they have used their freedom.

"Good Luck"

It's interesting to compare how the words "*mazal*" and "luck" are used in everyday language, especially when together with the word for "good." The former goes to the past, and the latter to the future.

Saying "*mazal tov*" in Hebrew is usually after something has happened. It's a way of praising someone for an accomplishment or event that's already taken place. In this case, it's about recognizing an achievement in the past.

On the other hand, when people say "good luck" in English, they're generally wishing someone well for something that's coming up, namely looking forward to a future event. *Mazal* and luck are opposites in this way: *mazal* is about what's already happened in the past or is happening in the present, while luck points to the future.

I think this difference shows something about how Hebrew speakers view external forces such as God in their lives. Saying "*mazal tov*" isn't solely about congratulating a person on an accomplishment. It may well also embody a recognition that something or someone (perhaps a higher power) helped make that accomplishment possible. Saying *mazal tov* not only applauds someone but also acknowledges the blessing that enabled their victory. It expresses thanks for it.

Perhaps the phrase "*mazal tov*" sends a message which relates to the duality of external and internal forces making good things happen. It's akin to saying: "you should be proud of your accomplishments, and also should acknowledge the help from on high to reach them." It serves as a reminder to work hard, but also a reminder not to become overly prideful or complacent, not to think the gain was all your doing, and not to take good things for granted.

In contrast to *mazal* looking backward in time, the Hebrew term for wishing someone well *before* an event בהצלחה (*behazlaha*) is more about active personal effort than external forces. In addition to hoping for luck to strike, it's also about wishing someone success based on what they do. The word itself implies moving forward or "crossing over," reminiscent of the Hebrews crossing the Jordan River to enter what became known as the land of Israel. *Behazlaha* puts in focus the individual's role in making things happen, rather than relying solely on external forces. It is about the power to exercise personal agency, as we'll see more in the final chapter of this book.

Giving Thanks

As we saw earlier, saying *mazal* is a way of expressing gratitude. It is a way of acknowledging a delight, whether it's come from yourself or from outside, whether from an internal or an external source. This method of expressing thanks can be seen as similar to a prayer. In prayers, people conjecture that God oversees everything and seek God's intervention.

People request that an external force influence their *mazal* to bring about a favorable outcome.

I heard this response to a situation where someone was saved in the war: ("היה נס, היה במזל, ברוך ה'")(*Haya nes, haya b'mazal, baruch Hashem*): "It was a miracle, it was a matter of *mazal*, blessed be God." In this context, *mazal* is seen as a gift from God, and the phrase acknowledges God's role in providing that gift. God is blessed for the blessing of *mazal*.

SOURCES OF LUCK

Where does luck come from, and who oversees it? One way to look at the word *mazal* is to trace its linguistic root to *nozel*, which means "to trickle" or "to drip" from above. This suggests that luck is something that drips down from a higher source, akin to a blessing from above. On this view, the source of *mazal* is external, something that comes from beyond us. It is thought to come from God, from the stars, or as seen in the next section, it may come from a person's own free conduct.

God

Many people believe that God is the driving force behind events in our lives. Since God is all-powerful, it is presumed that everything is part of God's plan. If luck and *mazal* happen, it is because God sent them. Later chapters will look more closely at how people see God's role in nature, science, and history. It's also important to note that God is seen as allowing humans the freedom to make their own choices. God is seen to be in partnership with humans in the ongoing process of creation and repairing the world.

Sometimes, when something unusual happens, people call it a miracle. Miracles are presumed a sign of Divine intervention. They are seen to be events that are caused directly by God.

While faith in God is generally associated with religious people, even secular people sometimes think of God as the force behind what happens and attribute to God events that occur. This is especially common in Israel, where secular Jews might say "It's all in God's hands," "With God's help," or "Blessed be God," even in everyday conversation. While in the U.S. these expressions tend to be the territory religious people, in Israel they are used by secular individuals too.

These phrases might help people cope with the uncertainty of life. They offer the comfort of presupposing that there is a reason behind everything that happens. Maybe it's not entirely that belief in God means that the believer presumes the control of a higher force; sometimes people use a religious-sounding phrase when they want to think that there is a reason that things happen. These sayings might reflect a desire for certainty, especially in defiance of the unknown.

Faith in God may be seen as pointing either to an external force or to an internal one. In Judaism, God is sometimes perceived as external, as separate from us. In the Torah, God is presented as *Other*. An example is the refusal Moses receives when he asks to see God's glory (Exodus 33:18–23). God responds that Moses can see God's back but not God's face. This emphasizes the Otherness of God. But in other parts of Jewish thought, including the spiritual tradition of Hasidism, God is seen as immanent, namely within both the Jewish people and the individual. Someone's faith in God is thought to bring God within that person. Also, on some views God gives individuals or entire communities a *telos*—a purpose, which becomes part of their inner being.

In a way ideology or values resemble faith in God. They can be internal or external. Such beliefs are internal psychological forces which shape how people think and behave and which drive them along. But they also create social, political, and legal structures which are external forces that make things happen in society. Morality works in a similar way: it is an internal conviction that guides our behavior, but also an external force that governs social conduct. These ideas are examined further in Chapter 4.

In Judaism, God is seen as a force insofar as God promotes human freedom, as well. God is in partnership with humanity; the two work together to shape the world. Creation started with God, but humans are given the responsibility to continue it. On the sixth day, God stopped creating, leaving the task to us. Human efforts are known as *hishtadlut*, which is key in Jewish teachings. The ongoing partnership in repairing the world, *tikkun olam*, is at the heart of Jewish thought.

A common question that arises in relation to the Holocaust is: "Where was God during the Shoah?" One response to this question is: "Where was humanity?" This emphasizes that God's partnership with humans requires that we take responsible action. We are not meant to rely passively on God to fix everything. Phrases like "It's all in God's hands" should not be used to suggest that we cannot or should not do anything. We are called upon to engage in the world and take responsibility for what we do.

This issue is considered in more depth in the final chapter of the book, where the importance of human agency and responsibility is discussed in relation to Divine involvement.

Stars

Some cultures believe that the stars are powerful forces which oversee our lives. The stars are deemed to instruct us how to behave, so that our lives will run in a good direction. But Judaism does not share this belief. The Torah expressly rejects it. A Torah passage records God saying not to follow the stars, not to follow the ways of other peoples (Deuteronomy 18:9).

There are three key perspectives on the stars in Jewish thought. First, the Torah forbids following the stars. Second, a Talmudic debate reveals that there is no star or constellation guiding the people of Israel. Third, a narrative Torah tale (a *midrash*) emphasizes that the stars can inspire us and be seen as a blessing.

First: The Torah specifically forbids looking at and worshipping the stars. In Deuteronomy 4:19, God warns:

> and lest thou lift up thine eyes unto heaven, and when thou seest the sun and the moon and the stars, even all the host of heaven, thou be drawn away and worship them, and serve them, which the LORD thy God hath allotted unto all the peoples under the whole heaven (JPS transl.).

The Torah forbids soothsaying and divination; the Jews are not to read the stars (Deuteronomy 18:10–11, Leviticus 19:26). The prophet Jeremiah echoes this by telling the Jewish people not to be frightened by the signs in the heavens, as the people of other nations are (Jeremiah 10:2).

Second: In the Talmud (BT-Shabbat 156:7 and BT-Nedarim 32a:2), there is a lengthy discussion about whether Israel has a star or constellation, known as *mazal*, that guides it. The conclusion of the discussion is that Israel does not have a *mazal*. This doesn't imply that we are unlucky. Rather, it emphasizes that our lives aren't directed by the stars. There is no star following us, or for us to follow, neither guiding us nor setting our future.

This aligns with the Torah's directive not to follow the stars or the Zodiac, as other nations do. It's worth noting, however, that archaeological findings including mosaics in the ancient synagogues in Tzippori and Beit Alpha show that in the practice of the people these rules were not always followed.

Third: While the Torah warns us not to follow the stars, it doesn't direct us to regard them negatively. In fact, stars can be seen as blessings. Such is the perspective in a narrative *midrash* (Bereisheet Rabbah 44:10) on the Torah passage where God tells Abraham to look up at the stars to understand how many descendants he would have. God wasn't asking Abraham to read the stars or rely on them for guidance, but to look above him: in the future, Abraham's descendants will be as numerous as the stars in the sky. A Talmudic Sage says that God told Abraham to look *up at* the stars: not to let the stars govern him, but to see how it all flows.

The stars are reminders of the blessings we have. Through them, the Torah suggests that God be thanked.

FREEDOM

People are themselves forces. The Torah shows Moses saying "It is not in heaven" (לא בשמים היא)(*lo bashamayim hee*)(Deuteronomy 30:12). This statement was made in the context of Moses assuring the Jews that Torah law is not beyond reach, not too distant or inaccessible. Yet the Talmudic Sages later use that phrase in the story of the Akhnai oven (BT-Baba Metzia 59b, described in Chapter 4) to show that we should not look to God for every answer. Rather, Jewish law is made by humans, through human interpretation. We can also understand that statement to say that it is for us to be the human agents, exercising freedom to move our lives ahead. This conception of human freedom is expounded later in the book.

In the Torah, stars are not seen as prevailing forces but as symbols of the power of human freedom. We observe them not in order to read our fate but to set the calendar. The Torah recounts how right after the exodus of the Jewish people from slavery in Egypt God instructs them to use the stars to determine the time and the seasons. In this way, stars are tied to freedom and human agency: it is free people who set their time.

The instruction not to read the stars suggests that there is no predetermined fate to uncover. This is unlike for instance in the movie *Serendipity* where fate seems to be something written in the stars, something beyond our control. Judaism teaches that the stars do not determine our path. We are free. This freedom is a gift, for which we give thanks.

Mazal can be perceived through the lens of freedom. Rather than understanding *mazal* as something dictated by external forces, it can be interpreted as a product of human freedom. In this sense luck is not something that happens to us. Rather, it is something we create through our decisions and behavior. *Mazal* can be shaped, as reflected in the modern expression of the Instagram trend promoting the notion of "self-made luck."

While I am not aware of a notion in Jewish heritage of a person making their own *mazal*, consider the term in modern Hebrew that is repeatedly used in contemporary speech הִתְמַזֵּל (*hitmazel*), as described above. This reflexive form of *mazal* suggests that luck has come about through someone's own conduct. Although the term literally means that *mazal* has brought itself to fruition, the use of the reflexive grammatical form is similar to how a person says they bathe or dress themselves. It implies that we have some role in bringing our own luck to fruition. We can, in a way, make our own *mazal*.

Mazal is a blessing, and the freedom to act is itself a blessing. We must acknowledge and give thanks for the gift of freedom and the opportunity it provides to shape our lives. Chapter 4 of this book further develops the idea that freedom is a force in shaping events. Judaism emphasizes this view, asserting that human agency is central to what makes things happen in the world.

CONCLUSION

We don't know where *mazal* comes from, or who controls it. Uncertainty is a human condition. What happens may be influenced by external forces such as God, the stars, or chance. Or it may arise from our own choices. What is clear is that it is not external forces alone that govern us. The free exercise of human agency plays a decisive role.

While we may never fully understand where luck is from, and who governs it, we can acknowledge and respect both the external and internal forces that bring it about. We should do our best to create our own good fortune, and be thankful for the blessing of freedom that enables us to shape our lives.

2

Chance

DOES CHANCE PLAY A role in forging the path in our lives? Is chance something outside of our control that makes things happen? Maybe the events in our lives are the result of random forces, similar to the roll of dice.

While chance might influence what happens, we really don't know much about it. We can't predict when or how it will strike, or what it will bring. Will it be good or bad? Like *mazal*, chance can be a delight or a threat, a blessing or a curse. Resembling the way there can be good luck or bad luck, there also can be fortunate or unfortunate chances. The randomness of chance is sometimes viewed as a positive sign, and sometimes not. Like *mazal*, chance signals the uncertainty we live with.

Chance encompasses not only happenstance but also probability. When we talk about "chances," we're often referring to the prospect of something happening. Interestingly, the Hebrew word *sikui'im* is often used both for "chances" and for "probabilities." In fact, modern science, especially quantum physics, shows that events are not utterly random but can be understood in terms of probability; they are governed by patterns and statistics.

In many religious and cultural traditions, people believe that God is behind everything that happens. Might God also be behind chance and probability? Could God be behind all the laws of nature, as philosopher Baruch Spinoza suggests? In Jewish tradition, occurrences are said to happen not exclusively by chance but under God's influence. Perhaps it is because of the uncertainty inherent in chance that people often attribute it to a higher power.

Yet humans too have a role to play in chance. Jewish tradition acknowledges that people can affect the chances they face. We can take risks, step into opportunities, and turn chance into something good or into something bad. We can shape chance into a delight or a threat. Chance is the result not entirely of external forces such as God or the stars, but also of human agency.

Taking a chance is never easy. Even though it's often encouraged, things don't always work out. In the ancient Roman classic *The Aeneid* it says that "fortune favors the bold." But taking a chance is also taking a risk. In Hebrew, the word meaning "chance" (*sikui*) is similar to the word for "risk" (*sikoon*). For example, in 2023, an Israeli Olympic reporter shared a story about a skydiving athlete who took a chance by jumping without knowing which way the wind would blow. Fortunately, the chance she took turned out to be to her advantage.

Why do people take risks? Answers vary. Some may believe that good *karma* or God's providence will go their way. Others might be testing these forces or hoping that fate or chance will align with their desires. Perhaps random or probabilistic chance will work out in their favor.

It also may be that a person's taking a chance or taking a dangerous risk is because their conception of the good involves a living-on-the-edge way of life. In choosing to take a dangerous risk they might feel that they're in control of their own story. It's an expression of agency, an active role in shaping one's life. We'll look more at the psychological factors behind our actions in Chapter 4. But here, the question under inquiry is not *why* people take risks, but *what* is thought to make things happen.

This chapter kicks off with a look at science, especially around the concept of time. We'll examine three forces at play: rules, God, and humans. In addition to humans reacting to chance, they can also influence it. They are involved in making chance happen. The next section shifts to Jewish tradition, focusing on the holiday of Purim and other holidays. Finally, we'll reflect on uncertainty, God, and freedom.

SCIENCE

This section explores classical Newtonian physics, which suggests that things happen in predictable, cause-and-effect ways and is perceived as having little room for chance, as well as modern quantum theory, which introduces a whole lot of randomness.

For a long time, philosophy was thought to have all the answers. It was considered the best way to understand *why* things happen and *when*. But then science took the spotlight. Science was believed to be the key to answering those same questions. Today, quantum physics has shaken things up by introducing the concept of randomness. It's not as if randomness was never considered before, but now it's become central to how we think about the natural world.

Previously, Newtonian physics introduced the concept of causation, describing cause and effect. In this framework, if you understand the cause, you can predict the effect. What then can we understand about the forces that control what happens? According to Newtonian physics, every cause has a corresponding effect. This fits with our natural instinct to look for explanations, to understand what makes things happen. People want reasons. In fact, the Hebrew word for "reason," *siba*, is closely related to *sibatiyut* (סיבה, סיבתיות), which means causality.

A famous example is an apple falling from a tree, a scenario often associated with Isaac Newton. The cause is gravity, pulling the apple as it falls. There is a tree before his college at Cambridge University which Newton is said to have sat under, making the story a bit of a legend. This example illustrates the Newtonian way of thinking about causality.

Another example is tossing a coin. Under Newtonian physics, a coin toss seems random. But, if you could control all conditions—the angle, height, speed, and weight of the coin—you could theoretically predict how it would land. This fits with the idea that with enough knowledge, you could predict the outcome of any event. It is a deterministic view of cause and effect, as defined by Newtonian physics. If you control the cause, you control the effect.

Yet the Newtonian assumption that every cause leads to a predictable effect no longer holds true in the realm of quantum mechanics. Quantum theory introduces randomness. In this realm, it's impossible to predict exactly where a photon or an electron will land. These particles don't have a fixed location; they can be anywhere. The belief that all conditions leading to an effect could be identified and controlled has been replaced by the understanding that randomness is everywhere in the universe. Modern science is all about uncertainty and unpredictability.

In quantum mechanics, the position of a photon or an electron is described by something called a *wave function*. This means we can't know deterministically exactly where the particle is, but merely the probability of where it might be. Once you measure it, though, the probability cloud "collapses," and you find the particle in one specific spot.

According to the Copenhagen interpretation of quantum mechanics, there are no hidden variables. That means the position of the particle is inherently unpredictable; it's not entirely that we don't know enough to predict it. If there were hidden variables, knowing all the factors would let us predict the outcome, namely, the particle's location. But quantum mechanics says that's not the case.

Still, quantum mechanics can help us make predictions, although without absolute certainty. It gives us probabilistic predictions, meaning it can tell us the likelihood of something happening. Probability helps us understand what has already happened, but it also helps us guess what might happen next. This connects with what was considered in Chapter 1, that *mazal* is about understanding the past, present, and future, offering insights about what has happened but also as to what's coming. In a way, statistics too are used to look at the past and then make predictions about future events based on probability.

Time

This relates to how we think about the flow of time. God is often deemed to be present in all directions of time. In the Torah, when Moses asks God what God is called, the response is "I will be what I will be" (Exodus 3:13-14). Interestingly, while this phrase is often translated as "I am that I am" in

English, the original Hebrew actually uses the future tense: "I will be what I will be."

That God interacts with all modes of time is further supported by the Hebrew name for God represented as YKVK. In Hebrew, the letters of this name are linked to the words for past, present, and future. That God is deemed to exist in the past, the present, and also the future is hence reflected in the text of the Torah.

God is also described as being able to "see" the past, present, and future all at once. This fits with a teaching from Torah commentary, where it's said that God sees everything in advance but still permits humans free will (as Rabbi Akiva explains in Pirkei Avot 3:15). This raises a key question; if God sees everything that will happen, how can we still have free will? One answer is that God sees all the possible outcomes, as with quantum theory, where all possibilities exist at once, but it's up to each person to choose which path to take. Another interpretation, from Elimelech Urbach in *The Sages*, suggests that God doesn't necessarily know every single outcome but observes everything unfold. We inquire into the conception of free will more in Chapter 4.

A question I put forward for others more knowledgeable in this field to consider is as follows: could causal influences work backwards in time, such as perhaps where time may flow backwards with antimatter? Quantum mechanics might then provide a way to understand a cause in the future producing an effect in the past. This raises the potential for a new form of determinism, in which the future influences the past.

The notion of time moving both ways—backwards and forwards, towards the past and towards the future—ties back to a point in Chapter 1. We discussed how in English, "good luck" is said before an event takes place, while in Hebrew, "*mazal tov*" is said after it has taken place. This difference could reflect time moving in both directions. It also ties into the concept of recognizing and giving thanks for the forces (perhaps God or spirits) that helped a good occasion come about. And it reminds us that human action matters; things don't happen by themselves, without our involvement. We again see the importance of giving thanks, and of exercising agency.

Time working in both directions could support the theory of quantum mechanics. In quantum theory, measurement helps to pinpoint the location of a particle, such as an electron, by collapsing the probability cloud. This assumes a kind of causal timeline. First, you measure, and then the location is determined. If time can move in both directions and God can see both past and future, then measuring and determining the location of a particle could actually affect its location in the past. This might lead to a new way of understanding causality in quantum mechanics, and show how much human agency matters in the process.

Forces

Under quantum theory, even without direct cause and effect and without being able to make exact predictions, there are three key things we can understand about forces.

Rules

First, even in the age of quantum physics, there are still rules that govern how the world works. The universe can be measured, for example, using statistical analysis. Statistics help us understand probabilities, and based on these, we can predict what might happen next. Probability resembles a rule that gives us an idea of what the future might hold. While statistics don't make things happen, they help us figure out what has happened and what may well happen next.

Though classical Newtonian physics is known for being deterministic, quantum mechanics can also be seen as deterministic, in terms of probability. Probability is a rule. It gives us a way to predict outcomes. Quantum mechanics can be considered deterministic in the sense that, once observed, we can pinpoint a particle's location; it becomes a known fact. That is, it can be determined.

Still, no matter what rules are at play, randomness is always part of the picture. Uncertainty is a natural part of life, and we have to learn to navigate the uncertainty that prevails in our world.

God

Second, maybe the rule of probability was set in place by God, or another external force. Some people think God created randomness as part of the way the universe works. Albert Einstein famously opposed the randomness of quantum physics. He famously said, "God doesn't play dice." He took the view that there must be hidden variables which, if we knew them, would allow us to predict outcomes. But modern theorists have found no evidence of hidden variables, meaning randomness really is a fundamental part of the universe. Maybe God put it there. Maybe God can be seen as having a role in chance.

Recognizing that there might be an external force at play can lead to gratitude. Many people thank God for the way things unfold in history. We'll dive into that more, later in this chapter.

Humans

Third, even in the world of quantum physics, we can still see the role of humans. But how is that possible, when outcomes can be predicted only as probabilities?

Humans, or the tools we create, can test these probabilities and devise tables of statistics. While the location of electrons or photons is controlled by a wave function, such that its location may be determined only once it is measured, the measurement itself can be done by a person or a human-made device. This suggests that our involvement plays a part in determining the outcome.

Take Schrödinger's famous thought experiment with the cat. The cat's state inside the box is unknown until the box is opened. And even after a measurement is made, the cat's state could change. Randomness is still at play. We need to accept uncertainty in the world and randomness in our lives. But we should also acknowledge that human agency plays a role in shaping outcomes.

In classical physics, but also even in quantum physics, humans have an effect. When you open Schrödinger's box, something happens. You are the cause, and there is an effect. It's not always predictable, and the outcome can change, but an effect is still triggered. We may not always know exactly what will happen, but we can decide on the cause, and in doing so, we can influence the effect.

Classical Newtonian physics allows you to be the cause and create an effect. Also in quantum mechanics, you can choose to measure or observe; you can set up a device that observes or measures. Or you can choose not to do so. It's all up to you.

The human role here is also collective. We're not solely individuals, but part of a larger group. Statistics, for example, aren't calculated on an individual basis. They are about groups, whether society, a nation, or even the whole world. What "happens" is about you in relation to others, not simply you alone. As we will see below, the Jewish notion of destiny is group-wide; it is about the destiny of the Jewish people, rather than about an individual's fate.

In the end, both Newtonian and quantum physics help us accept that randomness and uncertainty are a part of life, but they also remind us that individually and as a group humans play a key role in shaping the world around us.

JEWISH TRADITION

Chance plays a strong role in Jewish tradition. It is present in customs, the Torah, and Jewish commentary over the centuries. It has been an enduring presence in the lives of Jewish people, as experienced in the community across the ages.

This section takes a look at the holiday of Purim, followed by other Jewish holidays and traditions where chance has a part to play. We'll wrap up by reflecting on how Jewish teachings handle uncertainty, God's involvement in our lives, and human freedom.

Purim

At the heart of the Jewish holiday of Purim is the motif of a lot. The events of the time were to be fixed by chance. A lot, termed *Pur* in Hebrew, was tossed. But the holiday also illustrates God's role in shaping history and the freedom of human action.

Purim celebrates the time when the Jewish people in ancient Persia were saved from a wicked plot to destroy them. The name "Purim" comes from the word *Pur*, which means lot or lottery in Hebrew. The villain of the story, a Persian official, casts a lot to decide when to carry out his plan to wipe out the Jewish population (as told in the Book of Esther 3:7, 9:24). But the plan is overturned, and the Jews are saved.

Jewish tradition doesn't believe in fate the way the ancient Greeks did. As we discussed earlier and will return to later, Judaism rejects the view that a person's fate is predestined and unchangeable. This is clear in the story of Purim. What was supposed to be a tragic outcome, based on chance, didn't happen. The Jews were saved, and their fate was rewritten.

The Purim tale connects two important points: the forces of chance and the power of human freedom. The *Pur* (lot) symbolizes chance, namely randomness determining the fate of the Jewish people. But Purim also reflects freedom, as it marks the moment when the Jews chose to accept God's commandments willingly.

A debate in the Talmud questions whether the Jewish people freely chose to accept the Torah at Mount Sinai after the exodus. Some Sages argue that the Jews didn't have a free choice. They were hungry, thirsty, exhausted from slavery, and fleeing from the Egyptians. Yet the Talmudic debate is resolved by recognizing the Jewish people's free acceptance of the Torah at the time of Purim, marked by the phrase "fulfilled and received" (קימו וקיבלו)(*ki'imu vekiblu*)(Book of Esther 9:27, BT-Shabbat 88a).

While Purim is named after the lot (*Pur*) cast by the evil minister, the holiday has transformed into one of jubilation. There's a saying that joy comes with the beginning of the month of Adar, the month on the Hebrew lunar calendar on which the lot fell and the events of Purim unfolded. Purim is a time of joy, a reminder that even the worst fate can be changed.

Other Jewish Holidays and Practices

A key symbol of the Jewish holiday of Chanukah is the spinning top. Similar to quantum theory, where electrons can exist in multiple states at once, a spinning top can spin either clockwise or counterclockwise. The symbols of the spinning top of Chanukah and the lot cast on Purim recall the wheel spun by Vanna White on TV, and the spinning of a wheel of fate by the Greek goddesses known as the Fates. These images of women spinning the wheels of chance were brought up earlier.

A spinning top is a sign of delight in the *dreidl* game played on the holiday of Chanukah, which brings joy to people of all ages, especially children. The Yiddish word *dreidl*, and the Hebrew word סביבון (*sevivon*), relate to turning. The *dreidl* spins and it is not known upon which side it will land. Similar to the casting of a lot, it involves an element of chance and uncertainty.

According to tradition, it is the *dreidl* game that saved the Jewish people. In ancient times, when the Romans forbade the learning of Torah, Jews would pretend to be gambling by playing with the *dreidl* rather than studying Torah, in order to avoid detection. The Romans didn't harm them, and through this clever disguise the Jewish people were spared. Playing the *dreidl* game has become a symbolic practice demonstrating how luck can bring joy.

Another story tied to chance and delight is the Torah tale of Jonah and the whale, where lots are cast. Jonah tries to escape from God by boarding a ship, but a violent storm threatens to sink it. The sailors decide on a chance draw of sticks to figure out who's to blame for the storm, and Jonah's name comes up, suggesting that he's the cause. (The word for the lots on Purim and for Jonah is *goral*, which is discussed in Chapter 3.)

Today, in the U.S., Lotto is a big national game, much like the lots cast during Purim. In Israel, the government-run *Mifal Hapayis* lottery is also hugely popular. The Israeli government even conducts a lottery of reduced prices for new apartments, given the high cost of housing. This shows how deeply the idea of chance, similar to the idea of *mazal*, is woven into modern life.

Lessons

What lessons can we draw from elements of chance in Jewish tradition? The three points outlined earlier correspond to the three lessons I bring out here: Uncertainty, God, and Freedom.

First: Uncertainty

The first lesson is about how we deal with uncertainty. Modern science shows us that there's a lot we don't know and might never know. Uncertainty is a part of life, and randomness is built into the world we live in. It may be that there are causes of events which we don't know (epistemic) or there may not be any causes (aleatoric).

Tradition says that God set ten tests for the patriarch Abraham. One of these tests can be understood as dealing with uncertainty. In the Torah, God tells Abraham to take his son Isaac and offer him as a sacrifice. Abraham is instructed to travel to a place, "*hamakom*," that God will show him. As described above, Abraham doesn't know where he's going, but he trusts that God will guide him. He rises early, saddles his donkey, takes Isaac, and sets out, without a clear destination in mind. This moment is seen as Abraham passing the test of uncertainty. "*HaMakom*" is also one of God's names, and it is thought to represent the unknowns and challenges that come with having faith in God and following His commands, and which are part of life.

Second: God

The second lesson we can draw from exploring chance in Jewish tradition is the role of God in both chance and history. Chapter 1 recalled the Greek goddesses of chance, luck, and fortune. Here the focus is on God being seen as the force that moves history forward, guiding the destiny of the Jewish people. God is presumed to direct history, and for this, we are called to acknowledge and give thanks. Chapter 3 looks further into Jewish tradition regarding the destiny of the Jewish people.

The Hebrew word for "by chance" is *bemikre*. As we've seen, *mazal* and chance describe events that happen, and the root of the word *bemikre* is *karah*, meaning "happened." How does Jewish tradition view what has happened, and is it by chance? Torah commentaries suggest that events should not be seen as mere happenstance. Rather, God is involved in what happens in the world and in history.

The word "*mikre*" is examined by the former UK Chief Rabbi Lord Jonathan Sacks. When things happen, they are not to be considered to have happened by chance, or what is known as "*mikriut*" מקריות (from the same linguistic root). Instead, we should see them as part of God's plan. This is echoed in the *Shema* prayer, which assures that when the people follow God's law, rain will fall. In the Torah chapter *Eikev* it is emphasized that when we fulfill God's commands, good things follow not by random chance, but as a result of God's will. Rabbi Sacks draws on the commentary of the 12th century Jewish scholar Maimonides (Rambam) to illustrate this point.

Rambam calls for prayer and the sounding of an alarm when a bad event falls upon the people. This is instead of people attributing the event to happenstance, shrugging their shoulders and presuming that there is nothing to be done. Rather, effort must be undertaken.

Furthermore, Rabbi Sacks draws a distinction between *mikra*, a term for the Torah, and *mikreh*, namely an occurrence. Rabbi Sacks suggests that this distinction represents the difference between viewing history as a sequence of random events or as a story where God is guiding everything.

Torah texts point to God's influence at key moments in Jewish history. For instance, when Joseph reveals himself to his brothers in Egypt (Genesis 45:4–8), he tells them: don't worry that I will punish you for selling me into slavery; what you did, my brothers, was part of God's plan to save the Jewish people from famine. God uses Joseph's position in Egypt to ensure that food was stored and the Jews and many Egyptians were saved.

Similarly, the scroll of Esther (*Megillah*), which is read during the festival of Purim, recounts how God played a hidden yet crucial role in saving the Jews from destruction in ancient Persia. Although God's name is never mentioned in the scroll of Esther, God's presence is implied through subtle signs and hints. The meaning of Esther's name regarding hiddenness suggests God's concealed presence (*Hester*). God's presence is further implied through abbreviations used in the scroll.

Each of these examples of Torah text points to God's role in history, and also spotlights human action. Joseph and his brothers need to be active to stave off famine. Esther and the Jews need to be active to stave off destruction; Esther approaches the king unbidden, and she and the Jewish people pray and protect themselves. To this day, the Jewish people continue to mark the holiday actively with prayer and giving gifts to others. Indeed this point brings us to the third lesson to be derived from the approach to chance in Jewish tradition: Use your freedom to do something. Human agency is called for.

Even when God has a plan for the Jewish people, human action remains crucial. Mordechai tells his niece Queen Esther (Book of Esther 4:13–16): don't think that because you're in the king's palace, you're safe. If you don't act relief and deliverance (*"Revach Vehazalah"*) will come from another source, but you and your family will perish. This is a reminder that we all have a role to play.

This understanding of God's role in history aligns with Albert Einstein's view on treasuring coincidences. According to Einstein, coincidence is God's way of staying anonymous. Coincidence can be seen as part of God's hidden influence in history.

While God plays a role in history, the fate of the individual remains free, as will be seen further in the next chapter. People are still called to act, that is, to exercise their human agency.

Third: Freedom

The third lesson focuses on the Jewish tradition's belief in freedom and personal choice.

A joke tells that a man arrives in heaven and asks God: "Why didn't you grant me a lottery win?" God responds by asking: "Why didn't you buy a lottery ticket?" This well-known joke hints that buying a lottery ticket resembles taking part in what happens. The humor captures the essence of how human effort plays a role in *mazal*, and in chance.

In each of the Torah stories and Jewish holiday practices we've looked at, including Purim, Chanukah, and Joseph reconciling with his brothers, the human role is crucial. Even if God has a plan, individuals still have the power to make a difference.

Use your freedom to take a chance. Step into opportunities. It's not always easy. It takes inner strength, courage, and often a socio-economic support system to make it happen. An opportunity exists only if you see it as one, according to the Stoics. It all depends on whether you look at things as a good or bad chance, as good or bad luck, as the stars being behind you or blocking your way. The key is to act.

Humans need not be passive in the face of chance. We view it, but also influence it. And while we can't control every outcome and we bear the consequences of chance, probabilities, and risks, we're still responsible for how we engage with life's uncertainties. While bearing consequences isn't the same as causing an effect, the two are closely related.

Freedom and human agency are explored further in Chapter 4.

CONCLUSION

Chance is both a delight and a threat, both an opportunity and a risk, full of potential and uncertainty. Chance opens the door for both Divine and human action, by God or spirits or some external force and also by humans. Even where chance seems to take the lead, the Jewish tradition reminds us that both God and human choices are involved. As Mordechai tells Queen Esther in Persia and as Joseph says to his brothers in Egypt, everyone has a role to play.

Along with human freedom, ethics also matter. We're meant to use our freedom responsibly. People are to use their freedom to act responsibly, and with responsibility. This is so even with regard to chance.

The Hebrew word for probability (הסתברות, *histabrut*) is closely related to the word for reasonableness (סבירות, *sevirut*). This connection suggests that probability is not merely about chance, but about making reasonable decisions. It's a reminder to act responsibly. The Jewish tradition places strong emphasis on the duty of responsible use of our freedom.

3

Fate

FATE IS OFTEN PERCEIVED as an external force that governs the course of life and determines its endpoint. Fate is considered something dark, weighty, and inescapable. In Israel, the Hebrew term for fate *goral* (גורל) has gained prominence since the October 7, 2023 massacre. It seems to dominate the minds and hearts of everyone in Israel, and in Jewish communities around the world, who have lived through this difficult period. Yet Jewish tradition does not adopt the concept of fate. In Judaism, humans are believed to be free to forge their own paths in life.

Before October 7, the word *"mazal"* (luck) was everywhere. It was used all the time in media, in conversations, in everyday life. Since the attacks, however, the word *"goral"* has largely replaced *mazal*. What can we take this shift in language from luck to fate to mean? One response I heard is simple: on that day, our luck ran out.

Goral carries a more somber tone than *mazal*. It suggests something predetermined, inevitable, and often adverse.

Fate is seen as fixed, beyond our control. It is thought to be something we cannot affect through our own actions. In these days of war in Israel, soldiers, evacuees, and hostages all face a fate they cannot alter.

As one of my students pointed out, *goral* feels "heavier" than *mazal*. Another student of mine had a tattoo inked on her arm after the war began, reading *Amor Fati*, a Latin phrase adopted by Nietzsche that translates to "love of fate." This phrase suggests embracing fate as it is, even if it cannot be altered. In Chapter 4, this concept is contrasted with the notion of hope in Jewish thought.

The idea of a fate that's sealed at birth and can't be modified is common in Greek mythology. Take Oedipus, for example. No matter how hard Oedipus tried, he couldn't escape the fate that was foretold for him: that he would marry his mother and kill his father. In classical Greek (and Roman) mythology, the Fates (or Fortuna) spin the wheel of fortune, and where it lands spells out what will happen in a person's life. The Delphic oracle in ancient Greece predicted fates that were unavoidable.

But Jewish tradition offers a different point of view. Biblical Hebrew has no word for fate because Judaism does not conceptualize fate as inevitable, blind, or inexorable, as is explained by former UK Chief Rabbi Lord Jonathan Sacks. And as seen in Chapter 1, the Talmud doesn't mention any kind of heavenly star or sign for *mazal*, which could suggest that there's no such thing as fate at all.

In Judaism, we don't only try to escape fate, we create our own fate. Such is the concept of repentance, or תשובה (*tshuva*), which means that through our actions, we can alter our future. We change what we do, and as a result, change what happens and what will happen. Repentance is closely tied to the understanding of freedom in Judaism. Each person is free to choose their behavior and, in turn, shape their own life. How things turn out is up to them. Their fate is in their hands.

This chapter looks at the idea of fate through a few key lenses. First, we'll inquire into the meanings of the word *goral*. Then we'll move from words to images, exploring the icon of the spinning wheel, building on the discussion in the previous chapter of the spinning top in relation to chance. The third section refers to the individual nature of *goral* and the collective nature of the destiny of the Jewish people. This perspective will be revisited in the next chapter, especially in relation to current intuitions about destiny. Finally, we'll wrap up by discussing how freedom plays a central role in Jewish tradition, particularly in terms of making things happen.

THE WORD FATE / *GORAL*

Goral refers to the outcome or endpoint of a person's life. In English, based on the meaning it was given in classical Greek times, fate is often thought to be the force that controls the future. It cannot be avoided. Fate is believed to have been decided by a higher power, and nothing can be done to alter it. It befalls a person regardless of what they do. Yet the Jewish tradition underscores that the individual's fate is open, not fixed.

The medieval Jewish philosopher Maimonides (Rambam) writes that man's fate is not preordained (*The Guide to the Perplexed*, Book iii, Chapter 14). Humans are not bound by fate; rather, their choices are essential to the unfolding of their lives. There is always the possibility of repentance (*tshuva*): modifying your ways will modify where your life will go and also its ultimate outcome.

In Hebrew, the word *goral* is used for both fate and destiny, but there's a significant difference between the two. Fate refers to where the individual's life goes, while destiny refers to the collective future of the nation or people. In Jewish thought, an individual's fate is open and can be influenced by what they do, yet God has a plan for the destiny of the Jewish people as a whole.

In his book *Fate and Destiny* (the Hebrew title is *Kol Dodi Dofek*), the prominent 20th-century Rabbi Joseph B. Soloveitchik writes of *Brit Goral* and *Brit Yeud*: the Covenant of Fate and the Covenant of Destiny. In his view, the Covenant of Fate is informed by the historical experiences of the Jewish people's suffering, while the Covenant of Destiny looks forward with hope to the future. The difference between fate and destiny is returned to below regarding the individuality of fate and the collectivity of destiny, as well as in Chapter 4 of this book on lessons and hopes for the future.

The Hebrew word *goral* also refers to casting lots, a practice seen in several stories in the Torah. For example, in the Book of Esther, the evil minister in ancient Persia casts lots to choose the date for the destruction of the Jewish people. In the Book of Jonah, sailors cast lots to figure out who was to blame for the raging storm. The term also appears in the Torah reading on Yom Kippur (the Day of Atonement) where the High Priest of the ancient Temple casts lots to determine which of two goats would be sacrificed and which would be sent to the wilderness, symbolically taking on the sins of the people.

THE IMAGE OF A SPINNING WHEEL

Goral is often depicted as a spinning wheel, representing the cloth of life being spun. This concept is closely tied to *mazal,* and especially the Zodiac, called *galgal hamazalot* (גלגל המזלות), which literally translates as the "wheel of the constellations." The Zodiac, symbolizing the cycles of fortune, is also round and always turning. The connection between spinning and *mazal* or luck is reflected in the song "Luck Be a Lady Tonight," where the spinning of dice is tied to the notion of fate. On this approach, fate is determined by where the wheel stops spinning.

A spinning wheel also ties into the myths of Greek and Roman goddesses of luck and fate. In Chapter 1, we saw how the Greek Fates (the *Moirai*) are often shown spinning threads to represent the weaving of life's tapestry. The Roman goddess Fortuna is depicted with a spinning wheel, too. This imagery even shows up today in TV shows such as *Wheel of Fortune*, where Vanna White turns a giant wheel that determines the prize.

The image of spinning evokes the viewpoint that a fateful decision may result in a turn one way or another. Indeed fate, like a wheel, is thought to move this way and that, or to rise and fall. So too waves rise and fall, and the linguistic root of the word *goral* is closely related to that of a wave, both relying on the same Hebrew letters *gimel* and *lamed*. Hebrew phrases that describe fate as rising or falling such as עלה בגורל (the lot rose) or נפל הגורל (the lot fell) suggest that fate can go up or down, as does a wave.

Goral represents movement. Indeed there are ups and downs in life.

In the Torah, a lot dictating a *goral* is described both as rising and falling. For example, in the Book of Jonah, it says: "And the lots fell, and the lot fell upon Jonah" (Book of Jonah 1:7). In the Purim story, analogous phrases are used to describe a lot falling (Book of Esther 3:7, 9:24, with the term used to indicate the lot being cast linguistically similar to the word for the falling (הפיל פור)(*hepeel pur*),(נפל פור)

(*nafal pur*)). And in the Torah reading on Yom Kippur, the lot is said to rise on the two goats, as it is cast to determine their fates.

The image of a wheel being spun also comes to mind when the events of October 7 were described with Hamas conquering in the morning, but the Israeli Defense Forces (IDF) reclaiming territory by nightfall. The wheel reversed (הגלגל התהפך)("the wheel turned over"), and the outcome reversed.

Images of fate rising and falling also pop up in images depicting the war. Phrases such as "fate has risen" (עלה בגורלו)(*allah begoralo*) or "fate has fallen" (נפל הגורל)(*yarad hagoral or nafal hagoral*) reflect this idea that the outcome is unknown and always shifting.

Goral is akin to but also different from *mazal*. Akin to *mazal*, the word *goral* refers to something that will happen or has happened, but *goral* is considered a big deal. A Hebrew phrase הרת גורל (*harat goral*) means something momentous. The linguistic root of *harat* recalls a mountain, and also a pregnancy, both of which are certainly a big deal! The phrase signifies something weighty and meaningful. Relatedly, the term "a fateful decision" uses the term *goral* (החלטה גורלית) (*hachlata goralit*).

Also unlike *mazal*, which often refers to something positive, *goral* is typically associated with something negative. It carries a gloomy aura. *Goral* can be good or bad in the sense of laughter or tears. Phrases commonly heard are "laughter of fate" (צחוק הגורל)(*zhok hagoral*) or "tears of fate" (בכי הגורל)(*bechi hagoral*). But the phrase about laughter usually implies that fate is mocking someone. It suggests that someone is being poked fun at by the powers that determine their fate, rather than experiencing true joy. This contrasts with the way that *mazal* is often used, as seen in Chapter 1, as indicating a delight.

Goral reflects how uncomfortable people feel about not knowing what the future holds. While we want to believe we can control or predict how things will turn out, fate can be unpredictable.

Yet things can change. This concept is paramount in Jewish tradition, which rejects the conception of a fixed fate. Unlike the idea that fate is determined by a higher power controlling events, Jewish thought emphasizes that individuals have the power to shape their own path in life. Fundamental to the Jewish concept of freedom is the outlook on repentance: an individual can transform their ways, and hence transform their future.

INDIVIDUAL AND COLLECTIVE

In contrast to the ancient Greek concept of fate which suggests that our lives are already mapped out with a fixed endpoint that can't vary, Judaism does not embrace the concept of individual fate. In Jewish tradition, there is no belief that the life course of a person or its final destination is set in stone. In Judaism, each person has the ability to shape their own future. But the Jewish tradition has a conception of destiny for the group.

While Jewish tradition doesn't embrace the notion of individual fate, there is an idea of a destiny designed for the Jewish people as a collective. As Rambam writes in *The Guide to the Perplexed*, it would be a mistake to think that the movements of the celestial spheres are meant to control th fate of one single person or community. However, he does suggest it's possible they influence humanity's broader destiny.

In his book *Future Tense*, Rabbi Sacks discusses God's shaping the history of the Jewish people. Sacks underscores that while the concept of fate pertains to individuals, it takes on a collective form when applied to the Jewish people. This is evident in Israel today, given widespread concern about the fate of hostages, soldiers, and everyone in Israel as well as the Jewish people worldwide, who are impacted by events and sensitivities in Israel. We are said to share fate (שותפות בגורל)(*shutfut bagoral*). The idea of *goral* speaks to a collective destiny, that what happens to one of us happens to all of us.

The term *goral* is used to describe not only what has happened, but also what is yet to come and the ultimate end for the Jewish people. From this perspective, it represents a collective destiny, encompassing what is unfolding and what will unfold for all of us. What will happen to us is deemed to regard all of us, as a unified people. Defining and reaching the *yaad*—the destiny, the aim, the target, the purpose—is to be achieved collectively.

The next chapter will dive into how we can make that happen, focusing on initiative and action that is enabled by freedom. Where do Israeli Jews and the Jewish people think or hope that we are going? And what steps can we take to reach those goals?

FREEDOM AND HUMAN AGENCY

Throughout this book we have seen that human freedom plays a crucial role. You have the power to create your own *mazal*, your own luck. You can accept chances, seize opportunities, take risks, or choose not to. The same holds true for fate: you can form your own fate. Jewish tradition teaches that fate is not predetermined. The course of your life, and the ends towards which you aim, are largely in your hands.

Of course we have obligations, and limitations on our freedom. We have responsibilities to ourselves and to others, as well as restrictions on what we can do based on who and what we are and the circumstances surrounding us. But even within these confines, you have the power to shape your own *goral*.

The Israeli politician Yair Golan has contrasted two ways of thinking: one is about passively accepting your fate, which he connects to the experience of living in the Diaspora (Jewish communities outside Israel), and the other (which he calls the Zionist mindset) is about shaping your own future. He calls this taking ownership of your fate.

I often hear calls in these days of wartime to take our fate into our own hands: לקחת את הגורל בידינו (*lakahat et hagoral beyadenu*). This phrase captures the essence of personal responsibility, suggesting that one's fate lies in one's hands, rather than in the hands of others. This contrasts with, or complements, the approach of leaving everything in God's hands. One can remain grateful to God or external forces for affecting their life path, but still take personal responsibility for shaping it.

The message is clear: use your freedom in a responsible way. In my book *Positive Freedom and the Law*, I argue that freedom is duty. And to take action is a duty as well.

CONCLUSION

We are not controlled by fate; we have the freedom to make choices. This is especially evident in the current situation. Israel's enemies made the decision to start the war, and Israel, in turn, chose freely to retaliate. During a memorial service for fallen Israeli soldiers and Palestinians, it was said that war is not determined by fate but is a human choice.

Our *goral* is in our hands as a collective. In the midst of war, we can and must abide by the directions of the home command in taking proper shelter. God has given us the ability to act, and we must use it. There's an old saying: "God helps those who help themselves," and we have a duty to do so.

In the next chapter, we will explore freedom and human agency as forces that shape our lives, in particular in the Jewish tradition. We'll also look at the lessons we can learn from studying freedom and the forces at play in the situation of the current war.

4

Freedom

THE QUESTION WE BEGAN with was: what makes things happen? Is it the external force of luck (*mazal*), chance, or fate? Or is there an internal force of freedom at play? As we've explored throughout this study, freedom holds significant weight. We can forge our own *mazal*, chance, and fate. When we take action, we're the ones driving things forward. Our freedom means we can make things happen, and that we must. We're responsible for what we do, and we must choose and act responsibly.

Mazal, chance, and fate are terms used to describe what has happened, and what has made things happen. They provide us with reasons for events. We want reasons. We seek explanations for why things occur. The real force at work, though, is our power to choose.

Our freedom is not without limits. It's shaped by the things we care about, by our family, friends, and community. These influences, which I've discussed more in other works of mine titled *Positive Freedom and the Law* and *Freedom and Respect in Jewish Ethics*, can affect or even constrain our choices. Our freedom is also limited by the fact that we're human. For instance I can't fly because I don't have wings. That is a natural limit of being human. But even with these limits, we still have freedom. In the end, we're still the ones making the choices. Each of us has agency and can act.

Also our duties are inherent to our freedom. We have moral obligations to our family, friends, and community, and to the world around us. These obligations guide us in forging our path, and in doing what is right. Our responsibility is to choose the right path. When someone says to us *"Mazal tov"* or *"Yashar koach"* (ישר כוח), signifying that our strength is straight, we are blessed for having used our strength in the right way. We've made the right choice.

In Jewish tradition, freedom and responsibility go hand in hand. Rights and duties are bound together. We each have the freedom and the moral duty to act responsibly. Our freedom is the internal force that guides our actions. Rather than passively waiting for God or some other external force to take control, we must take responsibility. Our freedom allows us to exercise human agency responsibly.

In the next sections, we'll dig deeper into these ideas. First, we'll look at the difference between negative and positive freedom. Then we'll explore how Jewish tradition understands freedom, responsibility, and collectivity. We will also talk about what we've learned from this study, namely that using our freedom can be tough, but is also necessary. We'll discuss the importance of collective action and caring for others. Finally, we'll wrap up by looking at how people in Israel have responded to the current war with collective, responsible action, and what this means for the future of the Jewish people.

NEGATIVE AND POSITIVE FREEDOM

We are free to shape our own lives. This is a power that comes from within. It is an internal force. Liberal democracies allow us to do this, and Jewish tradition backs it up.

When we talk about freedom, people usually think of "negative freedom." This is freedom from interference by forces outside of us, as for example when the government controls your life. It is freedom from external forces that oppress you or force you into something.

We can think of freedom as being free from luck, chance, and fate. Those three elements are considered external forces restricting our freedom to act as we choose.

While negative freedom is about being free *from* outside interference, there's also what is called "positive freedom." This is the freedom *to* do things. Positive freedom is the freedom to act in ways that promote your growth and the fulfilling of your potential, termed self-fulfillment, self-realization, and self-actualization. With positive freedom we use our human agency to direct our life path. Agency refers to the execution of freedom through action; it transforms freedom into a lived reality.

The philosopher Isaiah Berlin, in his book *Two Concepts of Liberty*, explains positive freedom as the ability to control your own life. He asks who, or what, is the source of control or interference that can determine what you are to do, or who you are to be? With positive freedom, the answer is you. You are in charge of your life. You have freedom to make your own *mazal*, to take risks and step into opportunities offered by chance, and to direct your fate.

In his famous poem about taking one road over another, Robert Frost captures the essence of positive freedom. It's about making choices that lead to your personal growth. Philosopher Charles Taylor says that your positive freedom means your being the one who calls the shots in your own life. The more control you have over your decisions and your direction, the freer you are. Amartya Sen talks about freedom not only as about having the capacity to act, but also having the opportunities and resources that enable people to make free choices.

But how do we decide where to direct this freedom? We don't exercise freedom in a vacuum. We are all connected to other people, to family, friends, our communities. These relationships, or *attachments* as Taylor calls them, shape who we are and what we do. This is something a feminist perspective on freedom brings out, too. It emphasizes "relational autonomy," which looks to how our connections to others influence our choices, making us who we are and aiding us in figuring out what we want to become. Both internal and external forces mold our freedom.

When we look at the forces that make things happen, we see that both negative and positive freedoms are at play. Negative freedom protects us *from* external forces that interfere with our choices and actions. Positive freedom, on the other hand, is the freedom *to* decide what self-actualization means for us, to set our goals and to work towards them. In the end, freedom is about being your own force.

JEWISH TRADITION ON FREEDOM

Freedom is a key conception in Jewish tradition, encompassing both negative and positive freedom. It is reflected in how Jewish holidays are celebrated. A fundamental feature of freedom is human agency; we have the power to make choices, including when it comes to interpreting Divine law. The message that comes through is that as free human agents, we are called upon to act.

This section explores five main points: freedom as a core value in Judaism, the distinction between how Judaism looks at negative and positive freedom, how Jewish holidays emphasize freedom, the role of human choice in interpreting Divine law, and that we are meant to act as free people.

Core Value

Freedom is at the heart of Jewish thought. The Ten Commandments, recorded in the Torah as being inscribed in stone, underscore the significance of this value. The Sages of the Talmud suggest that the word for graven (חָרוּת)(*harut*) (Exodus 32:16) be read as freedom (חֵרוּת)(*herut*)(BT-Eruvin 54a). This highlights the notion that the commandments themselves are meant to bring freedom. Freedom is indeed inscribed deeply in the Jewish tradition.

The Torah spotlights freedom in its stories. In the Garden of Eden, Adam is given the task of naming the animals, symbolizing his freedom to choose (Genesis 2:19–20). Throughout the Torah, people interact with God freely. Abraham bargains with God to save the city of Sodom (Genesis 18:22), and Moses pleads with God on behalf of the Israelites (Exodus 32:9–14; Numbers 14:11–20 and 16:19–23). The number seven, which appears often in the Torah, is connected to freedom: the seventh day is the Sabbath, a day of rest, the seventh year is the Sabbatical year, when the land rests and slaves are freed, and the Jubilee year comes at the close of 7x7 years.

Another story from Genesis (4:7) shows God telling Adam's son Cain that he has the freedom to choose whether to do good or evil. Moses echoes this in Deuteronomy 30:19, when he reminds the Israelites that they have the power to choose life. A discussion in the Talmud (Midrash Tanchuma,

Pekudei 3:5) makes it clear that while God controls many things such as a person's physical traits, humans still have the freedom to choose between good and evil.

The exodus story, where the Israelites are freed from slavery in Egypt, is a major theme in Jewish tradition. It is recalled many times in the Torah text and in prayers. It's a reminder for Jews to never forget their history of being oppressed and hence to be sure not to oppress others, as seen in Exodus 23:9. This is an oft-repeated call for empathy and kindness to foreigners and strangers.

On Yom Kippur, the Day of Atonement, there's a prayer (*Ki Hinei K'chomer*) that compares people to clay in the hands of a potter, shaped by God's will. But repentance (*tshuva*) is available to everyone, all the time. The Yom Kippur prayers emphasize that repentance, prayer, and charity avert an evil decree based on a person's deeds of the past year.

Jewish tradition teaches that we couldn't be given commandments if we weren't free to choose whether or not to follow them. This approach is shared by the early Jewish thinkers Saadia Gaon and Maimonides (Rambam).

Negative and Positive Freedom

Jewish thought embraces both kinds of freedom. Being relieved from the burdens of slavery in Egypt thousands of years ago brought to the Jewish people negative freedom: freedom from oppression. After the exodus, this freedom enabled the Jews to exercise positive freedom: freedom to choose and act morally. They were free to stand in the desert at Mount Sinai and take on the moral law. Today, the Jewish people are seen as having both types of freedom: they are free *from* slavery (negative freedom), and also have the freedom *to* act as moral and responsible agents (positive freedom).

In Judaism, God's will and Torah laws aren't seen as restricting freedom. There are two reasons for this. Negative freedom isn't limited by God's presence because God isn't necessarily deemed a wholly external force controlling people. God is indeed seen as "Other"—as external and separate from human experience—for instance when Moses asks to see God's glory. Moses is refused, with God telling Moses that he can only see God's back (Exodus 33:18–23), taken to mean that humans can only perceive the outcomes of God's actions. Yet spiritual traditions such as Hasidism see God as more immanent, not completely separate from us. It gives a sense of Oneness with God, rather than Otherness.

Nor is positive freedom denied by God's commands. Rather than seeing God as a wholly external forcer commanding us, many in fact see Torah law as being in harmony with human nature because it is moral, rational, and compassionate. By living according to the commandments, people can align their behavior with their own values and morality, reaching their fullest potential. Many believe that following the Torah supports people in becoming their best selves.

Holidays

Freedom in the Jewish tradition is vividly reflected in the Jewish holidays. Take Purim, for example. It's a holiday all about freedom. Purim recalls that the Jewish people in ancient Persia were saved from an evil minister's plot to destroy them. In the Talmud, Purim is also seen as a time when the Jewish people freely accepted the Torah.

The Purim tale features both negative and positive freedom. The Jews' negative freedom was won when the wicked government minister did not succeed in destroying them. Also, they exercised positive freedom. The Jewish Queen

Esther courageously approaches the king to plead for the safety of her people, even though she wasn't invited to speak. Her brave decision to act helped to save the Jews.

The Talmud brings up an interesting question regarding freedom. In a Talmudic discussion it is asked if the Jews were truly free when they accepted God's commandments at Mount Sinai. The Jews were stuck in the desert, struggling with hunger and thirst, and surrounded by danger. They had just escaped slavery and may not have been in the right frame of mind to fully consider what they were agreeing to. One interpretation of the Torah passage that the Jews were at the foot of Mount Sinai is that the mountain was held over their heads like a barrel, implying that they didn't really have a choice. An argument brought forth is that to the same degree a debt that has been coerced may be voided, so too the giving of the Law at Mount Sinai should be voided because it was accepted under duress. As seem above, the Talmud resolves this issue by pointing to the people's free acceptance of the Torah in the days of Mordechai and Queen Esther, as related in the scroll (מגילה)(*megillah*) we read on Purim (Book of Esther 9:27), where it is written that the Jews "confirmed and accepted" the Torah willingly (קיימו וקיבלו)(*Ki'imu vekiblu*).

A similar theme comes up on Yom Kippur, the Day of Atonement. The Hebrew name, "Yom Kippur," can be seen as similar to—it is like ("*ki*")—the lot ("*Pur*") that fell on Purim. Tradition holds that on Yom Kippur it is decreed who shall live and who shall die, based on the person's deeds from the past year. Leonard Cohen's song "Who By Fire" touches on this view. But there's hope: people believe they can change the decree by changing their ways. A person's fate isn't set in stone; nothing is irreversible. Again and again in the prayer service it is said that repentance, prayer, and charity avert the decree. Both Purim and Yom Kippur see life as under God's guidance but still free.

The next sections explore how the emphasis in other aspects of the Torah on the power of freely taking action brings light into our lives. This recalls the verse from the prophet Isaiah calling us to rise and shine our light with God's light (Isaiah 60:1)(קומי אורי)(*koomi oree*).

Human Agency and Freedom in Interpretation

Jewish law, known as *Halacha*, is shaped by humans. The interpretation of Divine law from the Torah is done subjectively.

The Ten Commandments were given on tablets by God to Moses on Mount Sinai, said to be written by the "finger of God." But when Moses saw the people worshipping the golden calf at the base of the mountain, he smashed them in anger. Moses himself made the second set of tablets, which survived. Tradition says that Moses carved every letter. This is a key point: Jewish law was human-made.

And its development continues in human minds and hearts. There is a saying in Jewish thought that "the Torah has seventy faces," meaning there are many different and valid interpretations of it.

When the Jewish people first receive the Torah at Mount Sinai, they say "*na-aseh v'nishma*" (Exodus 24:7), translated as "we will do and we will hear." This wasn't wholly about following the commands, but also about giving them meaning. The modern Hebrew word for "meaning" (*mashma·ut*) shares the same linguistic root as the latter word the people say at Mount Sinai that they will hear (*v'nishma*). This links back to the perspective that meaning arises through human interpretation. At Mount Sinai the Jewish people gave their commitment both to uphold and give meaning to the Torah; in freedom, they would subjectively interpret God's word.

The practice of Jewish law is not entirely from heaven. It is not defined solely by the Torah, nor set exclusively by God. The Talmudic tale of the Akhnai oven illustrates this point. It shows Jewish law being determined through human interpretation, and God's approval of the process.

The Akhnai oven story in the Talmud (BT-Baba Metzia 59b) depicts Sages disagreeing about whether a certain type of oven is pure or impure. The brilliant scholar Eliezer argues that the oven is pure, and he is supported in his opinion by miraculous signs: a tree uproots itself, a river flows backward, and walls of the study hall begin to fall. A heavenly voice even calls out that Eliezer is right. Yet in upholding the majority opinion, Joshua quotes a Biblical passage stating "It is not in heaven!" (לא בשמים היא)(*lo bashamayim hee*).

The story illustrates that the interpretation of Jewish law is not for God to decide from above, but is up to humans on earth. The Biblical phrase (Deuteronomy 30:12) was used when Moses says to the people that the Torah is not far away, you can reach it. But the phrase has become associated with its meaning in the Akhnai oven tale: that Jewish law is to be interpreted by humans on earth, rather than dictated by God in heaven.

At the end of the Talmudic story, God laughs and says, "My children have defeated Me," showing that human interpretation of the law is accepted with jubilation by God. The Hebrew word for "defeated me" (*nitzhuni*) may indicate the everlastingness of God recognizing that the interpretation of Divine law is to be in human hands on earth, not by God in heaven.

Since the time of the Talmud, Jewish law has continued to evolve through human interpretation. As the 20th-century Rabbi Joseph Soloveitchik says, it's about autonomy. It shows our freedom to interpret and decide for ourselves.

Another way to understand the phrase *lo bashamayim hee* is that one's life path is in one's own hands, not God's. It is not that everything that happens is "*maktub*," a term used in Arab cultures to indicate that what is written is set to happen. It is not an external force in the heavens that makes things happen, far away in the distance. Instead, *lo bashamayim hee* can be taken to mean that life is shaped by our own agency, by the internal force of human freedom. I've written about the phrase *lo bashamayim hee* and the idea of human freedom in my article "Choice and Obligation," in *Mesorah Matrix* on *Jewish Thought and Spirituality: U-Vacharta ba-Chayim*.

As with Jewish law, we have the freedom to interpret the world around us. The meaning of things is in our hands, not dictated by something far away. In my work I've explored what art means, and what Torah means. For instance in art, because satire states falsehoods it has faced complaints of libel. Yet I believe that its meaning comes from how readers interpret it. And the meaning of art should be allowed to evolve over time, rather than being locked in place by copyright law. Similarly, the meaning of Torah and Torah law should be given the meaning understood by readers. In both cases, I'm drawn to the idea of the freedom to create and interpret meaning in what we encounter in life.

Ultimately, the power to define meaning lies with us, not with some distant force, but is in our hands.

Act

There's a strong emphasis in Jewish tradition on human freedom and power to make things happen. We are to use our freedom wisely to shape the world around us. The Torah includes both positive commands (things you should do) and negative ones (things you should avoid): do and don't do. It is said that the positive commands are harder to follow. We are to act.

In the early chapters of Genesis in the Torah God creates the world, and after six days ceases creation. The Torah says that humans were made in God's image. Commentators explain that echoing God's being a creator, so too we are to create. Echoing God's being free—with the freedom to cease creation after 6 days—so too we are free.

A popular story in the Torah depicts Abraham being commanded by God to get up and go: to leave his father's house and homeland and head towards what would become the land of Israel. The Torah chapter is named for the words of that command, *Lech Lecha*, meaning go with (or for or to) yourself. A similar name is given to a later chapter in the Torah, *Vayelech*. It has the same takeaway: get up and go.

This conception is different from the concept of *amor fati* that Nietzsche made famous. That is a concept about embracing our fate, accepting whatever comes our way. The Torah perspective is also unlike the Greek myth where Sisyphus keeps pushing the rock uphill forever with no hope of change. Judaism is all about movement, progress, and hope.

Rabbi Akiva states: "Everything is foreseen, yet freedom of will is given" (Ethics of the Fathers (Pirkei Avot) 3:15). One way to understand this is that while God knows all possible outcomes (like the many possibilities in quantum theory), it's up to us to choose which one to pursue. Our decisions are in our hands.

We're partners with God in creation. While the Torah says that the creation of the heavens and earth ceased (Genesis 2:1), a passage in the Talmud suggests that people finish the job (BT-Shabbat 119b). We are to complete creation and repair the world. This concept is known as *tikkun olam*. For instance, in the book of Isaiah the prophet talks about our responsibility to feed the hungry and care for the poor (Book of Isaiah 58:6, 10, and 12). The partnership with God is also reflected in the Kiddush, the blessing over the wine on Friday night: God made the grapes, but people make the wine.

A great example of this partnership is the *midrash* story of Nachshon ben Aminadav. When the Israelites were fleeing from slavery in Egypt and reached the Red Sea, the waters blocked their way. Nachshon was the first to step into the water, and only then did God part the sea. The lesson here is clear: we need to take the first step, even if it's uncertain. Begin moving, without waiting for everything to be set for you.

Another story from the Torah about the time when the Jews were slaves in Egypt involves the king Pharaoh's daughter reaching out her hand to save baby Moses from the water. He had been abandoned there because of Pharaoh's command to kill all male Jewish babies. While God aided her, it was her action that made the difference. This reinforces that we're meant to take action, even when it seems as if "it's all in God's hands."

It is sometimes asked: where was God in the Holocaust, the *Shoah*? A response often heard to this question is another question: where was man in the *Shoah*? In other words, people had the responsibility to take action. We had a duty to stop it.

A joke sums up this outlook. A man is stranded on a sinking ship and refuses all rescue attempts: boats, floats, and helicopters. When he dies, he asks God at the gates of heaven why God didn't save him. God replies: "Why didn't you take the boat, the float, or the helicopter?" The joke emphasizes that while God plays a role, we also have responsibility to act. The power to act comes from within us. The force making things happen is internal.

The theme of taking action even in the face of uncertainty is reflected in the Hebrew phrase *be-hatzlacha* (בהצלחה) used to wish someone well before an event. It carries a more active meaning than "good luck." It comes from the word *tzalach*, meaning "to succeed" or "to cross over," encouraging proactive engagement. The word is used to refer to the Israelites crossing the Jordan River thousands of years ago to enter what became known as the land of Israel.

Jewish tradition also teaches that with providence God guides us, but the guidance isn't about passivity. The concept of God's personal providence (השגחה פרטית)(*hashgacha pratit*) sometimes suggests that God is involved in each individual's well-being. But this doesn't mean we are to sit back and wait for God to make things happen for us. We are to make an effort (השתדלות)(*hishtadlut*). The relationship we have with God, called the Covenant (ברית)(*brit*), allows for our growth and development. A Hasidic interpretation even suggests that what happens on earth impacts the higher spiritual realms as well.

Maimonides (Rambam) teaches in his *The Guide to the Perplexed* that while in providence God extends care for us (Book iii, Chapter 18), our actions still have a major impact. Providence depends on our striving for perfection and intellectual development (Chapter 14). Providence isn't automatic; it depends on us striving to be the best version of ourselves. Hence it is our responsibility to act, and responsibly so.

Responsibility in Judaism

Freedom is not solely about doing whatever we want; it is also about recognizing that we are responsible for our actions and have the responsibility to care for others. After the exodus from slavery in Egypt, the Jewish people stood at Mount Sinai and in their newfound freedom took on the moral law. This is the duty to the Other, namely to respect

God and other people. In this section, we'll look at the connection between the Self and the Other, freedom and responsibility, morality and collectivity.

Self and Other, Freedom and Duty

In Jewish tradition, freedom and duty are always connected. They go hand in hand. Freedom is about the Self—the individual—but also about the duty to the Other—to God, and to other people. Freedom gives a duty to act responsibly and with responsibility to care for others. The Hebrew word for responsibility, *ahrayut*, comes from the linguistic root *aher*, meaning "other." Responsibility is essentially about being aware of others and responding to their needs.

Being responsible means looking out for the safety and well-being of others. A classic example from the Torah shows this in a command to build a guardrail around your roof (Deuteronomy 22:8). Why? To prevent someone from falling off. In the Talmud, there's a discussion where Sages ask: if God wants someone to fall off the roof, they will fall; why build the guardrail? The answer given is: to be sure that no one falls off of *your* roof. The esteemed 10th century French Torah commentator Rashi teaches that the commandment is meant to ensure that everyone takes responsibility for avoiding someone's injury or death. A person has the choice of whether they build the parapet (guardrail) or not, and the choice either to do the right thing or face the consequences.

I discussed responsibility at length in my book *Freedom and Respect in Jewish Ethics*. In beginning work on that book I would ask people "What in your view is the central value in society?" I found that many responses surrounded the Self (self-expression, self-actualization, self-realization, choice) and also the Other (compassion, caring, doing good for others, and contributing to society). One's selection of values is what one tries to adopt to guide their life. People's intuitions about central values are about Self and Other.

I also talked in that book about how to show respect for others. I called it affirmative behavior; it is about seeing, hearing, listening, and acting to support them. Start with looking at the other person. Hear their voice. Listen to them. Talk to them. And care for them.

A key part of respect and responsibility is compassion, or *rahamim* in Hebrew. There's a story in the Talmud about Rabbi Akiva's daughter being saved on her wedding night from a poisonous snake bite, because earlier that day she gave her wedding feast to a poor man (BT-Shabbat 156b). In Jewish tradition, some believe that the compassion you extend in this life can affect your future lives. This approach is similar to *karma*, the belief in many Asian traditions that what you do in one life will come back to reward or haunt you in subsequent lives.

The theme here is to act responsibly, and to care for others.

Morality: Doing What's Right

It is generally seen as being responsible to act in a moral way. It is seen as being responsible to do what's right. Morality brings people to care for Self, and for the Other. Is this an external or an internal force? It can be seen in both ways. Insofar as it is internal, it reflects freedom: a person's choice to act in the right way.

Living morally is often described in Jewish tradition as following a straight path. Saying "*yashar koach*" is a Hebrew phrase that means "well done" for using your strength in a straight way. Morality guides us down that path, and can be thought of as a force that pushes us to do the right thing.

It has been explored throughout this study whether forces deemed to make things happen are external or internal. External forces may be from above, and anyway outside of a person's control. Internal forces come from within us, and are something we can control. Morality can be seen either as an external or an internal force.

Some argue that moral law is externally imposed by God via the commandments in the Torah, or by society's laws and customs. Jewish law (*halacha*) is an example of this. In addition to rules being what is said in the Torah, the rules of Jewish law are passed down through tradition, often shaped by rabbis or by what the community deems acceptable. A society's code of ethics is often understood to be constituted by customary social behavior.

Where moral law is set according to the community's ethical code, namely what people in the community do, it is internal—to the community, and to the people living in that community. Morality can also come from within an indiviual. It can be what someone believes is right or wrong.

There's a middle ground, where morality is seen as something universal that comes from human reason. It's based on what's logical or reasonable, and even though it comes from within each individual, it is also thought to apply to everyone. Acting with reason or being reasonable is often thought to be responsible. In my first book *Positive Freedom and the Law*, I explored this conception both through the lens of Immanuel Kant's philosophy and Jewish tradition.

Akin to morality, ideologies can be either external or internal, coming from either outside or inside us. Some ideologies are passed down worldwide, or by society or culture, while others come from within the individual. The philosopher GWF Hegel theorizes that ideas move through history; they move things along and make things happen. But even ideas that move through history can come from within. An ideology may be an internally-derived set of ideas or beliefs. For instance, Marxism is an ideology shared among workers around the world, but a Marxist theory also can arise from a person's internal moral system.

A person might believe they have a *telos*. This may be deemed their natural end, their purpose in life, their *raison d'etre*. One's belief in their *telos* may function as a strong force in the person's life. It may drive them to move towards a specific end or purpose, and hence to make things happen. Does that belief come from something external or from inside of them? Some might think of a person's *telos* as coming from God or the universe as an outside source, while others might see it as something they've developed themselves.

Law is an example of a social structure that makes things happen. It is a source that may be external (from an external authority) or internal (in a democracy, based on self-determination). Moreover, it may be founded upon ideologies and beliefs and morality. The legal theorist Ronald Dworkin argues that law itself is an expression of morality, and law puts moral principles into operation in society. Such moral principles may be based on a society's ethical social codes and hence considered external, or internal notions of reason and our understanding of what's right and just (whether that's individual or universal). Either way, whether law is an external or internal force, law is often seen as setting the right way to act, and following the law is often deemed as the right thing to do; it is considered being responsible.

To the degree that moral and legal principles arise from a social code, they reflect collectivity. This brings us to the following discussion: of the collective freedom and duty to do what's right.

Responsibility doesn't fall exclusively on the individual, but is collective. It's about working together to do what's right.

Collectivity

Freedom in Jewish tradition isn't uniquely about individual rights; it's also about collectivity. Jewish teachings value both the Self and the Other, accentuating how important it is for people to interact responsibly. Freedom is something to be exercised together, not alone. Jewish tradition teaches to show responsibility, collectively.

In the ancient text Pirkei Avot, the Sage Hillel is famously quoted as saying: "If I am not for me, who will be for me? And when I am for myself alone, what am I? And if not now, when?" The first part speaks to individual freedom, reminding us that each of us is a human agent. The second part reminds us that freedom isn't solely about "me," but about "us." It underscores the importance of others and the need for collectivity. And the final part is a call to immediate action.

Our connection to others is a form of collectivity. As we've seen, the Self is not atomistic and independent. Individual freedom isn't a solo experience, but is shaped by family, friends, and community. Many of the limits to our freedom come from the relationships and social structures we're part of. Our choices aren't made in a vacuum; they're influenced by our surroundings.

We also have duties to others. Our behavior affects the community, and our responsibilities are wider than for ourselves. Lessons regarding climate change and democracy are two of the examples discussed below which show our duty to take responsible action, collectively. Climate change is a global challenge that requires the involvement of all of us. Also as to democracy, we have to think not entirely about our own personal freedom, but about the impact we have on our society, and on the world.

Coming together as a community is echoed in the famous line from Psalm 133: "Behold, how good and how pleasant it is for brethren to dwell together in unity!" The verse lauds the beauty of harmony and togetherness. It has become an acclaimed song.

Another renowned saying in Jewish tradition is: "All the people of Israel are responsible for one another" (כל ישראל ערבים זה לזה)(*Kol Yisrael arevim zeh lazeh*)). This approach to mutual responsibility reinforces the perspective that while people are individuals, they are always connected to others.

Collectivity can also be seen in the Purim holiday, which emphasizes the responsibility we have to each other. In the Purim story, Queen Esther works towards the good of all the Jewish people in the ancient Persian Empire. Even today, the holiday is observed with delivering baked goods to neighbors (called משלוח מנות)(*mishloach manot*), and the giving of charity. The Purim scroll (מגילה)(*megillah*) is read together with other people in the community. Similarly, Jewish prayer is done collectively, in a group of ten, known as a *minyan*.

Jewish tradition also underscores collective responsibility when it comes to sin. On Yom Kippur the community recites together a list of sins. The phrasing is always: "The sins which we have committed . . . ." Responsibility for the sins is shared. We are all free, and we are all accountable for each other's sins.

The idea of collectivity will be returned to later in the book, in the exploration of the lessons we can learn from this tradition.

IT ISN'T EASY

Agency can be tough. It's not always easy to find the energy or the courage to take action, to get up and make things happen. Taking responsibility isn't effortless, either. In fact, freedom can sometimes make people anxious.

When we feel as if we're in control of everything, it can be overwhelming. Suddenly, we're carrying the weight of every decision and its outcome, which can be a lot to handle. When we name an external force and hence blame something or someone outside of ourselves, perhaps God or another power, we don't have to take accountability for what went wrong, and we don't have to deal with the consequences.

Also freedom itself can feel like a burden. If we see freedom as self-actualization, it comes with the pressure to discover and be true to the "real me." Setting big life goals can add even more stress as we try to figure out how to reach them.

Religion can add its own set of pressures, too. Many people feel the need to follow specific religious rules or practices, or heed religious leaders. Others consider themselves pressed to live up to an ideology, whether it's one they've chosen or one their family or community holds. And the pressure to do what's seen as the "right thing" in terms of morals can feel burdensome.

Psychological Burdens

Freedom is a burden in a further way as well. The psychologist Eric Fromm, author of *The Fear of Freedom* (1941), saw the rise of fascism in Europe in the 20th century as a response to people's fear of the freedom that democracy brought them. According to Fromm, for many people democracy left them feeling empty. They missed the sense of belonging, identity, and meaning that came with being under the control of powerful institutions like monarchies.

But liberal democracy, at its core, actually offers people those things. It's built on values that people hold dearly. Those values give them belonging, identity, and meaning. Belonging comes from people in a liberal democracy feeling connected to others who value freedom and work for the same goals. Living in a democracy gives people a perception of identity, not merely as individuals, but as part of a free people. And freedom itself offers meaning, as it allows individuals to exercise their rights and have control over their lives.

In addition to being free from restrictions, freedom is also about having the power to shape your own life and your future. This positive freedom gives people a feeling of belonging, identity, and meaning. It's about having control over your life, which ties into who you are and where you belong.

These psychological factors are internal forces causing people to exercise human agency. Yet they are drives—the internal forces that motivate people to act, what moves people along—rather than what people say to explain what makes things happen. This study will continue to concentrate not on the reasons people take action, but on their intuitions about what makes things happen. And in this chapter, the focus is on how freedom affects people's deciding to make an effort.

One way to address the fears around freedom is through the spirit of community found in Jewish tradition. Jewish culture has always placed a strong emphasis on collectivity, and facilitates individuals' feeling belonging and identity. For generations, people have identified with their Jewish community and the Jewish people as a whole. The tradition provides for many people meaning, including when it comes to freedom.

In Israel, these values are very much alive. Israelis often see themselves as part of a collective, and they define their identity through their connection to the nation and to the broader Jewish community. This appreciation of collective belonging offers them an identity and a deeper meaning in their lives, and bolsters their feeling grounded.

We can see this now, in the midst of war. While of course war itself is never something to extol, the responsibility, collectivity, and shared commitment to the nation's well-being has been remarkable. This dynamic will be explored in more detail below.

LESSONS

There are important lessons we can take from the way freedom is understood in the Jewish tradition. One lesson is that we're meant to embrace our freedom, be grateful for it, and recognize the forces both inside and outside of us that shape the world around us. But here's the key: we can't simply sit back and let things unfold. We have to act. And we must use our freedom responsibly.

It's easy to think that things are out of our control. But we are not to shrug shoulders, lift hands and say "there's nothing I can do," assuming that whatever happens is meant to be. If our leaders are heading in a direction that worries us, it's our responsibility to step up and make a difference. We have a duty to do our part to protect the world we live in.

The instances of climate change and democracy show why effort is necessary. Later, we'll talk about these issues and also about the ongoing war and what it teaches us about stepping up when it matters. The main takeaway is this: whether it's protecting the environment, defending democracy, or responding to crises, we all have a part to play.

And when we work together, we're stronger. Efforts in each of these areas display the importance of immediate and responsible action, but also the power of coming together. Working together, to protect our freedoms and fulfill our responsibilities, we can make a difference. For example because climate change is a problem that impacts everyone, the solution needs to be a collective effort. Similarly, the fight to protect democracy is rooted in collective self-determination. It is a form of general will. And as we'll explore later, the ongoing conflict Israel faces further underscores the strength of unified operations.

Climate Change

Let's begin with climate change. Formerly called global warming, climate change is no longer thought to be exclusively about rising temperatures, but is about extreme weather events such as heat waves, droughts, floods, and more. Instead of accepting it and thinking, "this is how it is, and there's nothing we can do," we need to take action. As the saying goes, "God helps those who help themselves."

Some people argue that higher temperatures are part of a natural cycle and that humans haven't significantly contributed to it. But that opinion is in the minority. The overwhelming scientific consensus is that human activity has had a huge impact on the planet's changing climate. Ethics point to upholding the truths propounded by scientific evidence, as I talk about in my previous book, *The Ethics of Truth*.

Regardless of whether we are or aren't the ones who have caused climate change, it doesn't mean we should give up on trying to prevent it or at least slow it down. We still have the power to change things. Human behavior can influence the outcome. Even if the changes we are seeing to the climate are part of a bigger, uncontrollable picture, and even if they are determined by luck, chance, or fate, our conduct can push things in a better direction. The Torah tells us in Genesis 2:15 that it is humans' job to "work and protect" the earth. That is exactly what we should be doing now.

Democracy

Next, let's talk about democracy. Consider the Israeli government's efforts in recent years to overhaul the regime. The ruling coalition has attempted to strengthen the executive branch of government at the expense of the judicial branch. Protests erupted across the country, with people standing up to protect their democracy. The number of people who poured into the streets to protest the overhaul was enormous, and the protestors made a difference. But the fight isn't over; it still needs to continue.

Some argue that if regime change is what the majority wants, so be it. But majority rule is not equivalent to democracy; it is a tool for making sure that power lies with the people. And when we talk about "the people," we have to include minorities, whose rights must be protected. Democracy works if everyone's rights are respected, not merely those of the majority. Some members of Israel's ruling coalition have been critical of the Supreme Court for standing up for minority rights. But protecting those rights is what keeps democracy solid.

The road ahead is long. Building a stronger democracy and a fairer society won't happen overnight. But we can't let up. We all have a role to play in keeping the momentum going. Responsible, collective, affirmative behavior must be robust. Everyone's involvement counts. As Alexis de Tocqueville pointed out, democracy relies upon civic engagement.

In response to the governing coalition's attempt to change the regime in Israel through a judicial overhaul, a protest group I helped form named *Revach Vehazalah* was inspired by the approach framed by Mordechai when he told his niece Esther, who had become Queen in ancient Persia, if you don't do anything the well-being of the Jewish people will come from somewhere else. Even when things seem out of our control, we must do something.

The War

Lastly, we can't talk about lessons without regard to the recent war Israel faces. The horrors of the massacre that was brought upon the Israeli people beginning on October 7th, 2023 were unimaginable. Yet the way the Israeli people have responded shows the power of freedom.

People came together right away. They have volunteered to aid families who lost loved ones or had relatives taken hostage. They have assisted the many Israelis who were evacuated. They have supported the country's defense efforts. They worked to find ways to improve the situation, in Israel but also in Gaza and around the world.

We'll further examine the war situation by asking: was it a matter of luck, chance, or fate? We'll see that in fact it has illustrated the role of freedom, of human agency, of collectivity, and of responsibility. From there, we'll explore destiny, and even how children are getting involved in activism.

THE WAR

Mazal, Chance, Fate—or Freedom?

The ongoing war between Israel and seven neighboring Arab entities has been a subject of study throughout the book. Was it a matter of *mazal*, chance, or fate? Rather, I argue, it speaks to the strength of freedom.

Mazal? This time, we lost our *mazal*. One Israeli I spoke with said: "Our luck ran out." And while *mazal* is often good, this time what happened was bad. Sometimes, people use the word *mazal* as if it's mocking us, playing with us, laughing at us (המזל צוחק עלינו)(*hamazal tzohek alenu*).

Chance? No, the war wasn't a random, chance event. Hamas planned it for years, and Israel should have seen it coming. Israel could have been more prepared and called up soldiers sooner. Nor should the return of the hostages be left to chance. We need to bring them home now.

Fate? Some people talk about the war as if it's the result of fate, something out of our control. Yet what happened wasn't due to a natural force that could not be avoided. It is about Hamas in Gaza assaulting Israelis, and about Israel failing to respond quickly enough to defend civilians and mobilize soldiers.

The war is often considered an endpoint, as fate or *goral* is. It spells out what has happened, where the lives of many have gone: of hostages, soldiers, and the nation. Yet what will happen is not set by an inescapable fate. Through freedom and human agency we can make a difference. At the rallies for bringing the hostages home it is underscored that this is a time for people to pour into the streets.

The term *goral* is used quite often now in Israel, during the difficult times of the war. People are scared of a bad fate and uncertain of what's to come. But Nietzsche's concept of *amor fati,* accepting fate without trying to change it, goes against the Jewish and Israeli mindset. Israelis are in movement, rather than accepting whatever comes their way.

Freedom? One of the essential features of freedom in Jewish thought is the emphasis on taking action. This approach is clearer than ever during the war, with Jews all over Israel and around the world stepping up to assist.

An Israeli from Emek Yizrael spoke of protecting himself, and owning up to his responsibility. His safety depends on what he does, not on luck, chance, or fate. He's taking charge of his situation.

Israel's protection may be coming from an unseen external force, such as God or the stars. But it also comes from within people; it is what they do to protect themselves and each other. Israeli society is to be applauded for its efforts. One Israeli said after one of the many bombing attacks on Israel: "It's not *mazal* that saved the bomb victims from harm. It's following safety instructions, going to sheltered areas."

People express gratitude to external force(s) that are thought to have been supportive. People also show gratitude to humans undertaking efforts that matter. Some thank God for creating human beings with freedom and the power of agency. Perhaps we're working with God's help, but the responsibility is ours. As the Jewish tradition teaches, after creating the world, God rested on the seventh day, leaving the rest to us. It's up to us to act.

Collectivity

We're seeing that freedom is not *solo*. It isn't something we experience alone, but is about collectivity. In this time of crisis, people are coming together, working as one, whether it's for the military or in civil work.

Numerous civil efforts have been taken. People are assisting those who have been hurt in the attacks, and offering aid to those evacuated from towns in the north and in the south near the frontlines. Defenders of Israel engage social media to respond to all of the fake news about Israel. Many visit soldiers who've come from abroad to join the army, far from their families. Many, many Israelis go to funerals of fallen soldiers, cook meals for displaced families, and support soldiers in need of assistance. Everyone is taking a part.

This spirit of collective action is rooted in *arvut hadadit* (ערבות הדדית), meaning mutual responsibility. A popular slogan seen on posters everywhere in Israel says: "Together we will win" (*beyahad nenaze-ach*). A frequent saying on banners and shirts at the rallies for bringing the hostages home is a message to the families of the hostages: we are with you, you are not alone (*anachnu eetchem, atem lo livad*) These slogans reflect the strong sense of solidarity that's assisting people in making it through this difficult time.

Israeli athletes at the 2023 Olympics in France spoke of how they were channeling their emotions about the war into their performances. They were striving to be the best athletes they could be and proudly representing Israel, standing together, holding the Israeli flag high. Also beyond Israel, the Jewish community worldwide is standing together.

The collectivity seen at this time challenges the fear of freedom suggested by the philosopher Erich Fromm. Israel's collective efforts show how people are overcoming that fear. By acting together, they create belonging, identity, and meaning.

Act Responsibly, and Take Responsibility

Responsibility is about taking responsible action and also about being accountable. Arguably many in the Israeli army, government, and citizenry right now are doing their best to respond responsibly to the current crisis, although not everything has gone perfectly. And the leaders who were in power at the time of the tragedy of October 7 and the war that followed need to acknowledge their accountability for what has happened and is continuing to happen.

DESTINY

Consciousness of destiny is a strong element in Jewish thought. In Hebrew, the word *goral* is often used to indicate both fate and destiny, though they are different. While fate is seen as something inevitable and individual, destiny is about the collective future of the Jewish people as a whole. Rabbi Soloveitchik, in his book *Fate and Destiny*, writes of Jewish tradition holding that God has a plan as to where we are headed. Destiny is something the Jewish people are working toward, in partnership with God.

In the Biblical narrative of Joseph meeting his brothers in Egypt, Joseph reassures his brothers that what they did was part of God's plan. Even though they sold him into slavery years before, it was because Joseph was in Egypt and attained a high post that he could save his family from famine. God has a plan, but it's up to people to play their part in making that plan a reality.

Today, many Israelis are reflecting on their country's destiny. What does the future hold for Israel? What is the future of the Jewish people? This question recalls the question I posed to people for my book *Freedom and Respect in Jewish Ethics*: what in their view is the central value in society? Now, in the midst of this onerous war, for many it is survival; staying alive is the central concern. But there are also hopes for peace, equality, and a better future. Before the war, many spoke of peace with the Palestinians as a goal, hoping for a shared future living side by side. But now, with everything that's happened, that seems less likely in the near term. Still, world peace is something that people continue to dream of. Hope remains alive.

There's also a lot of frustration in Israel over inequality when it comes to military service. Many ultra-Orthodox religious Jews, known as Haredim, don't serve in the army, even though they receive public subsidies supporting them all through their lives. While the Haredim are allowed to study Jewish texts instead of serving in the military, many don't even do that. This enrages Israelis, especially now at a time of war when many are required to perform military reserve duty for hundreds of days per year. Many of the soldiers in combat on the front lines, who are away from their families and jobs for months and months, feel bitter when they see Haredi men who are physically fit but not contributing their share to the society. It's estimated that around 63,000 Haredi men could serve but don't, and only about half of them actually study Torah.

I point to perspectives on destiny to underscore the feelings of Israelis during these trying times of war, but also to show their hopes. Despite everything, people are still holding on to the belief that we can work together to build a better future.

We can act collectively and responsibly to bring about peace and equality in Israeli society. Even in these dark times, hope can keep us moving forward. Having a vision of what we're working toward, and what we can do each day—whether it's something small, like cooking for soldiers, or something bigger, like building a fairer society—can keep spirits up. Knowing what we can do and staying active helps us to keep going. But also holding onto a long-term consciousness of where we hope we will go, what type of Israeli society we hope to achieve, is beneficial.

Discussions about long-term goals for Israel started long before the war. History shows that in the last years of a state's first century, internal conflicts often arise as people try to figure out the country's future direction. The United States, France, and Russia are examples of this. Even in ancient times, the Jewish people's periods of sovereignty lasted around 75 years. Many believe now is the time for Israelis to explore where they want the country to go, and together to work towards getting us there.

Especially in times of war, soldiers need to know what they're fighting for, but it's the same for all of us. The Israeli government often talks about strength, but for many people, the real goal is to uphold values such as justice, freedom, and respect. These values are not solely about surviving, but about creating a society that reflects the values.

Justice was a core value for the Biblical prophets, as we see in the Torah and as is stated in Israel's Declaration of Independence from 1948. Freedom and respect are also paramount in many Israelis' intuitions about values. Freedom is a right but also a duty of respect for others' freedom and for who they are.

Many also think about the kind of society they want Israel to be in the future. There's a desire for integrity, honesty, and uprightness. These values have been shaken by political corruption but remain pivotal as to what many Israelis hope for. "Yosher" (integrity) is a value that comes up often in discussions about the destiny of the nation. And it is one we can work towards, together.

Even in the face of war, it's crucial not to lose hope. In the kibbutzim along the Gaza border, which were devastated by attacks, people are already starting to rebuild. There's a notion that if they can do it, the rest of us can too. And even after the horrors of the Holocaust, survivors sang *Hatikva* (התקווה), meaning hope. This spirit of resilience can guide Israel through these tough times.

LITTLE ACTIVISTS

Taking action to work for change can begin at a young age. We all know that students can be powerful agents of change, but even young children can have a big impact. We've seen young people lead global movements, like the Swedish climate activist who has inspired millions.

I remember when I was little sitting at the kitchen table with my father as he would write letters to lawmakers, urging them to take positions on certain issues. I would join my Dad at protests on Sunday mornings in front of the Russian Embassy in New York City, calling for the right of Jews to emigrate from the Soviet Union. As a student, I marched in Washington DC with my Mom and friends for women's rights. It is common in Israel for parents to bring their kids to protests to teach them the importance of standing up for what's right, as indeed I did with my kids.

I hope to encourage readers of all ages to think critically about the world around you and to express your opinions on issues that matter.

CONCLUSION

Freedom is about more than having the right to make choices; it's also the duty to take responsibility for those choices and for the world around you. In Jewish tradition, freedom means carving out your own path. It's about making the most of the opportunities that come your way and working with others to build a better future. Even in the darkest times, we can act responsibly and collectively. Together, we can create the destiny we hope for.

Concluding Remarks

WHAT MAKES THINGS HAPPEN? What forges our path in life? We do. We have negative freedom *from* interference with exercising agency, and positive freedom *to* act. With our freedom, we have the power of human agency. Forces are often thought to be out there, determining what will happen, controlling us. But freedom is an internal force that allows an individual to take control over their direction in life. Your luck, the chances you take, and your fate are all within your control, or at least open to your influence. It's up to you to make things happen.

Of course we can't control everything. But we can—and should—use our freedom to act: affirmatively, responsibly, and collectively.

Isaac Bashevis Singer once said, "We have to believe in free will: we have no choice." We are grateful for our freedom, and for the ability to make things happen.

While we each have the freedom to choose, we are never truly alone in defining who we are. We're influenced by others, and by the world around us. And it may be believed, as Rabbi Jonathan Sacks points out, that we accomplish nothing without both our efforts and God's help. We are partners with God. That is the meaning of the Covenant.

*9 7 9 8 3 8 5 2 5 1 7 5 9 *